THE
CHAPLAIN:
Fighting the Bullets

"For we wrestle not against flesh and blood, but against principalities, against powers, against rulers of the darkness of this world, against spiritual wickedness in high places."

(Ephesians 6:12)

THE CHAPLAIN:
Fighting the Bullets

" . . . Father, forgive them; for they know not what they do . . . "
(Saint Luke 23:34)

CHARLES E. GROOMS

Ivy House
Publishing Group
United States of America

PUBLISHED BY IVY HOUSE PUBLISHING GROUP
5122 Bur Oak Circle, Raleigh, NC 27612
United States of America
919-782-0281

ISBN: 1-57197-375-3
Library of Congress Control Number: 2002101707

Hardcover edition: 2002
Paperback edition: 2003

Printed in the United States of America

Major General Stanhope Spears
Adjutant General of South Carolina
Courtesy of SCMD/TAG

DEDICATION

I dedicate this book to a loyal supporter of chaplains, and my friend, Major General Stanhope Spears, the Adjutant General of South Carolina. He is not only a friend to chaplains, but also a friend to all veterans that served and are serving in the armed forces of the United States of America. General Spears is the Commanding General of the South Carolina Army and Air National Guard, and has the distinction of being the *only* remaining elected adjutant general in the United States. He is responsible for the men and women that serve in the South Carolina National Guard, the Air National Guard, the South Carolina State Guard, the Joint Services Detachment, the National Guard Support Operations, and the South Carolina

Disaster Preparedness Division. Under his leadership, when these units have been called upon to serve the state and the nation, they have distinguished themselves above and beyond the call of duty.

It was my privilege to have served as a Battalion and Brigade Chaplain in the South Carolina State Guard under the command of the former South Carolina Adjutant General, Major General T. Eston Marchant. General Marchant did an outstanding job promoting the reactivation of the South Carolina State Guard in 1981, and took steps to provide the needed readiness training that would prepare the State Guard to respond adequately if activation became necessary. However, when General Marchant retired, Brigadier General Stanhope Spears ran and won the election to become the new South Carolina Adjutant General. Upon becoming the adjutant general, he was elevated to the rank of Major General. General Spears has continued to build the South Carolina military department into a first-class command. His wisdom, leadership, dedication, integrity and patriotism have earned him the reputation of being one of the best adjutant generals in the United States. It has been my honor to have served as a chaplain under his command, and to experience firsthand his loyal and faithful support of the military chaplaincy.

TABLE OF CONTENTS

DISCLAIMER

First, it is necessary to understand that an individual contemplating a chaplain career in the United States armed forces (including the Army, Air Force, Coast Guard and Navy, as well as the Air National Guard and the regular National Guard or Reserves) must, once approved, attend an official military chaplaincy school. *Therefore, the data contained in this writing is for informative purposes only!*

Second, the writer has taken the officially required duties and responsibilities of a chaplain and organized them into a format easily understood in layman's language. Personal interviews conducted with active duty chaplains, retired chaplains, and personal experiences gained by performing chaplain duties and responsibilities as battalion chaplain, brigade chaplain, deputy staff chaplain (office of the Chief of Chaplains), Chief of Chaplains (South Carolina State Guard), and Chaplain Advisor for Religious Affairs (Joint Services Detachment, Office of the Adjutant General of South Carolina, South Carolina Military Department) served as a reservoir of information to be referred to in writing this book. The historical references in this book are summarized from information recorded in books the author studied in college on United States history. In addition, military statistical data was reviewed via research conducted on the internet (Department of Defense government archive files), in military field manuals, such as FM 22-5 and Chaplain Activities 2A Pamphlet 165-3, and in historical accounts recorded in the Bible.

This book has been written as a guide for individuals seriously considering entering the chaplaincy, either as a volunteer or as a paid chaplain (civic and veteran organizations, medical facilities, law enforcement, corrections, veterans administration (VA), civil air patrol, volunteer state defense force or state guard military command under the official command of a particular state's adjutant general).

Every effort has been made to make the book as complete and accurate as possible. There may be mistakes, either typographical or in content. Therefore, the material is to be a recommended general guide for interested persons. The author shall have neither liability nor responsibility to any person regarding any loss or damage caused or alleged to be caused directly or indirectly by the information contained in this book, and it is in no way a replacement for official military manuals.

FOREWORD

Inexperience and lack of training often hamper the practical everyday work of the chaplain. Formal courses of study provide for a foundation upon which to build, and experience gives the student the opportunity to explore and use what he or she has learned. The problem with experience is that it is a hard taskmaster and many times too rigid. This book, *The Chaplain: Fighting the Bullets,* as presented by Chaplain Brigadier General Charles Grooms, takes us steps forward in the learning evolution of being an effective, positive and successful chaplain.

From his experiences and the experiences of many he has served with come this excellent guidebook. Wisdom is the application of knowledge. Having applied the knowledge he has obtained over the years, and having experienced what many chaplains will someday experience, he has made the road to success easier for us by sharing his experiences through the development of this guidebook. We can experience it ourselves or we can extract the wisdom of one who has. This we can learn by applying the principles and precepts so clearly presented in this edition. This guidebook is highly recommended to all chaplains, and to those who aspire to be a chaplain or who would like to work as an assistant in the chaplain's office.

In His service and yours,
Chaplain Major Dewey E. Painter, Sr.
USN Veteran (Ret) / Wing Chaplain, Florida Wing, CAP

PREFACE

There were several things that prompted me to write this book, *The Chaplain: Fighting the Bullets*. There are many important reasons for writing this book, such as recommending guidelines that would provide assistance to those individuals thinking about a volunteer or active duty chaplaincy ministry, regardless of where their selected work "pulpit" would be, or what religious denomination he/she would hold their credentials. But, to be more precise and honest about it, the history of chaplains reflects that chaplains have always had to fight to exist in the military.

The chaplain's fight is not against individuals with real bullets. The chaplains' enemies use bullets made up of slanderous and discriminating words, evil tactics, religious faith group persecution, favoritism in promotions, et cetera. Even though the bullets are not real bullets, nevertheless they kill off good chaplains. The military is not the only place where religious warfare is waged. Chaplains/clergy have to battle religious wars within as well as without. It is what I refer to as the "Trojan Horse Theory" (A theory I came up with that definitely backs up my personal evaluation of chaplains/clergy, denominational practiced prejudice in high places, and among some so-called Christians . . . "destroying one's brother/sister in the Lord from the inside of the religious circle of Christians with jealous attitudes and gossip"). Improving one's educational credentials and advancing to leadership positions resulting in rank advancement (promotions) in the military, be it active duty or volunteer military service, does not make an individual any better than anyone else or more important. But, some weak-minded individuals become jealous, and interpret and perform a self-analysis of those accomplishments as an individual thinking he/she is more important and just showing off. They should be encouraged to get "off their backside" and improve upon their educational status to be able to promulgate the gospel more effectively and affluently . . . "study to show thyself approved." Sad, but it's so true. One must get over that type of idiotic behavior, and grow up in the Lord!

Prepare yourself in the warfare of fighting the bullets. One other very important fact that is intended to serve as food for thought, and as hard as it may be to believe, is that the "bullets" will not only come from line officers and noncommissioned officers, but will come from fellow chaplains desiring to get ahead. They will conspire against each other to get better assignments and to be promoted. So, my friend, prepare yourself for psychological warfare. The fight to be a chaplain requires more than just a desire; it takes guts, grits, spiritual determination and dedication to the calling in order to pass the test.

The information contained within has been gathered utilizing research study materials and actual personal experience as a military chaplain, a prison warden, a highway patrolman, a chief of police, a juvenile services' administrator, four consecutive years as National Chaplain of the State Guard Association of the United States, and thirty-nine years experience as an ordained minister, chaplain, evangelist, pastor and interim pastor. And, I have not learned it all! But, I have been there and done that!

Another reason surfaced when several people I had never met before, along with many friends of mine, began to listen more closely to some of my brief testimonials about my background and varied experience gained by having served in so many "people service" oriented positions. Their comments, encouragements and recommendations to me were interesting and thought provoking, such as, "You should consider putting your life's work into book form, it could help others." After much prayer, many long hours toying with the idea, plus an unbelievable number of requests received from individuals requesting chaplain study materials, I finally decided to become one of many people who have chosen to try and make a difference by writing of their experiences.

In addition, I decided shortly after becoming a Christian that I would not be shamed in any manner, by anyone, because I believed in and followed the principles and precepts communicated to me from the four gospels of the New Testament: Matthew, Mark, Luke and John. That same spirit has followed me throughout my Christian life, even into my chaplaincy career, and has surfaced quickly, especially when so-called evil forces attacked the validity of God and Christ, my religious faith group and my personal integrity. I exhibited and followed what had been engrained in me as a United States Marine—*Marines don't retreat from a fight*. Do not become a coward! Advance to a better position, and stand your ground! You are trained to become a man.

That attitude may not be the best way to go, but standing up and defending the reputation of my Lord, my faith and my honor seemed to be a justifiable reaction at the time . . . let the chips fall where they will. Looking at it from a military standpoint . . . you must be willing to pay the price. Sometimes promotions or transfers will be the payback for a reactionary! But, what the heck, I liked to fight for an honorable cause.

A "biting the bullet" attitude is one of the most recommended suggestions from friends and counselors! But, for me it has been a different situation. I have elected to "fight the bullets."I have spent most of my chaplaincy career fighting for what is right. Standing up for the underdog! Asking pinpointed questions! Demanding equal justice and fairness! Going against political favoritism in high places! I dare to say, cowards have fired their bullets from sniper positions, but fighting the bullets off has given me an unbelievable following, a silent booster club. I know who they are, and the Lord does, too. And, I honestly believe the Lord has been behind the scenes promoting my career promotions for having the courage to stand up! Fighting the bullets will cause wounds (promotions, transfers and career changes, et cetera), and even at times there will be death (retirement, early out, bad assignments, reduction in status, et cetera). If you find yourself giving up, becoming weak-minded, or feeling scared to stand your ground, dodging the bullets will be almost impossible. Some ministers and/or chaplains just *are not* leaders; they are followers. Which are you? Don't rock the boat is the order of the day.

Yet another reason, more important than any of the others, sprang out and touched my heartstrings . . . helping veterans. Veterans—they have been trained by the military to fight, kill, drink and obey orders, and once the war or their military career is over they are sent home to live out the rest of their lives productively as family men and women. As I personally evaluated more closely the thought placed in my spirit, and reflected back on the lives of veterans I have known—especially those in my family genealogy, including myself—facts were revealed that those veterans, at least a high percentage of them, ended up so affected by their entrenched military lifestyle that nobody could tolerate them . . . sometimes not even themselves. Family life was destroyed. Divorce was imminent and followed close behind. A job could not be held down. Financial difficulties entered all of their lives. Children suffered as a result . . . families were torn apart. What actually happened was that the veteran became a worthless nobody in the view of his own family, and in his own view. The veteran was in and out of court and jail! The town drunk or drug addict. The beggar on the street. The sight I saw with my spiritual eye would not go away! They are not able to fight off the bullets of alcohol, drugs, battle fatigue, old age, and divorce! Help is needed.

Veterans are, without a doubt, the most neglected human beings in the United States of America, and if it could be adequately researched, this statement could probably describe veterans from around the world. If you think about it from a serious standpoint . . . the lifestyle that all Americans enjoy, such as freedom and liberty, free expression, government support programs, war around the world but not on American soil, opportunities to obtain the American dream and many more items you could add to the list, were paid for in military persons' blood. Why? All because of what our veterans did to preserve this American way of life. Did it cost anything? Yes, it sure did . . . the lives of our military personnel . . . disabilities and homelessness in most cases.

The wounded returned from harm's way to try to adjust their lives, believing that America would take care of them for their sacrifices . . . fighting to protect every citizen's freedom in the United States. But, it has not been an easy way; it has been a long, hard battle just to exist! The wounded have not recovered . . . the wounds are only getting worse, and age has crept in to compound their problems. This only refers to medical difficulties; it does not speak to living conditions and the cost to live . . . money! Living expenses just to survive are a tremendous worry that brings on stress and pressure . . . resulting in strokes and heart attacks. "What the hell," (excuse the French) some may state, "if death occurs, it's just another veteran we don't have to worry about." Garbage! It's a disgrace and an indictment upon our American way of life regarding taking care of our veterans. Promises by the United States government to take care of its veterans are slowed down by the bureaucratic paper mill, unfair counselor evaluations and decision makers that are non-veteran themselves and most of them communicate an attitude of "don't care."

Just as an example, let's do a comparison between inmates and veterans:

I've spent twenty-eight years in the correctional and law enforcement career field, with twenty-one of those years as a correctional administrator. During this same period of time I was a military chaplain (S.C.M.D./TAG). Therefore, as I review the comparison between inmates and veterans, the general information really disturbs me greatly. And, it should also upset you as well! The comments I am about to refer to are documented facts gleaned from my personal experiences on the job.

Why is it that we have so many inmates confined to prisons throughout the United States who are being taken care of better than our veterans? The inmates are given free medical treatment, food, shelter, educational and job training opportunities, hygiene items, clothing, televisions, recreational programs, room and board with air conditioning in the summer and heat in the cold months, well furnished up-to-date libraries, and, at the same time, their families are provided for adequately! On top of that many inmates are paid "some amount of money" for their labor! Who pays for it? The government!

The inmates take advantage of the system while serving their incarceration by becoming physically fit and educationally smarter. The "smarter" inmates, so they think, learn how to sue the system and bog down the courts with unjustified paperwork. Once they get out of prison and return to society their muscle-bound body language communicates a psychological forced threat on people implying they can "whip up" on law-abiding citizens of all races, and even law enforcement officers, and without fear. These types live in a revolving door cycle . . . in and out of prison all of their lives!

Why are our veterans, men and women that have gone to war and served their country honorably, being denied the same benefits given to inmates and their families? I cannot really understand the reasoning behind "elected" officials in government being so callous. I am talking about those elected officials who are holding the purse strings, making decisions and treating our veterans differently than they do inmates! I cannot figure out who to blame! Maybe the government officials are not veterans themselves . . . that could possibly be one of the reasons. I guess we are to blame! If we are to blame, then what are we going to do about it? Inmates fight for their rights; why don't we veterans do the same?

Unless we veterans band together as one voice, things will *not* get any better! The same old tune will continue to be sung! We need strong lobby voices in our cities, counties, states and in Washington to keep up with our elected representatives. Vote them in, and if they don't look out for the veteran's best interest equally in comparison to others in society . . . vote them out. But, to do that we must organize into a unified group and initiate a strong frontal attack. Members of the American Legion, Disabled Veterans, VFW, and so forth must band together to speak as one voice to our elected officials. A "Custer's Last Stand" or a Normandy-type landing is in order. The purpose is to stop the unreasonable treatment of veterans.

Are inmates more deserving than veterans? NO! Heck no! But, inmates must be held accountable for their criminal behavior, and at the same time inmates should be treated in a decent and humane manner. If the inmate cannot do the time, then don't do the crime. Society pays the bills! And, at the same time, the government must be held accountable for their neglectful treatment of veterans in granting deserved rights and benefits. Pressure must be applied to the system to stop treating veterans any old way. Anything less is unacceptable!

One of a few ways to get some action is to continuously call or write your elected representatives—be it city, county, state or your representatives serving in Washington. Look in the blue pages of your telephone book to get telephone numbers of city, county and state representatives. For contacts with your representatives in Washington call the Capital Operator free at: (877) 762-8762, (877) 788-9001, or (888) 762-8768. Ask the operator to connect you to your senator or congressman. Once you make the contact, express your concerns . . . and then be a thorn in their sides by passing it on to other veterans and asking them to do the same!

Believe me when I tell you this will work if it's a total veteran effort; it will get results. Believe me, it will!

There is one conclusion. It is often stated, "If you cannot depend on the minister or the chaplain to stand up for you, who then can you depend upon?" They represent God, His Son and the Holy Spirit, and should be interested in winning souls! Veterans have souls, too. I am a missionary-minded chaplain and a supporter of missionary work; please do not misunderstand what I am about to state. It is hard for me to personally understand how we pastors, churches, businesses and individuals, will gather funds to send missionaries and materials outside of the United States, to people and places around the world, and to people we do not know (these are absolutely needed areas), but, we will not do the same equally to help people we do know that live down the street and around the corner within our own communities, especially to help our veterans and their families. *We should take care of our own first!* Now, please don't label me an unreasonable person because I make these statements. I only ask you to look into the mirror with me and see what you see! We see the person that could make a difference! The truth needs no defense . . . it will stand when the world is on fire!

Help to get the veteran through the red tape of government. That can be arranged through assistance programs. Veterans helping veterans. What to do? How to do it?! Constructing military records! The government cannot start the helping-the-veteran process without verifiable military records. Most veterans do *not* have these records. The delay is misunderstood by most veterans, so let's *help* them! As a chaplain I want to reach out to the veterans and their families and provide assistance as best I can, but another motive enters the picture. Restoration to a faith in God . . . winning them unto the Lord. This is the "gap" I must stand in. And, if you are interested in helping veterans as you say you are, then you are invited to stand in the gap with me! A person is only as good as his word. A coordinated program/ministry can be set up and become a veteran's "refuge center" for help. We're working on such a place right now! View my website—*www.veteransoutreachministry.com.*

So, you see the title, *The Chaplain: Fighting the Bullets*, had many reasons behind its development. I wrote primarily to reach the souls of people, especially veterans and their families. You *help* 'em first. They will be puzzled about why you do what you've done for them without a catch to it! At that point, you can "witness" about the Lord's love, grace and the purpose behind your ministry. Maybe it will bring about results, and maybe not . . . but, you have tried! When we talk about helping veterans and their families, we *include* everyone. The family genealogy of people, more often than not, includes someone that is or was a veteran . . . no person is left out. Our mission is to reach out to veterans and their families. If you care about veterans, become a partner and get on the team!

The personal history I have shared with you was not noted to impress a single person. It is a fact that veterans are dying by the thousands daily, and many are leaving the world unprepared to meet God favorably. As a chaplain and minister, I bury many veterans that have departed without the saving grace of Christ. That concerns me, and it should concern you as well. One must prepare himself or herself by establishing a strong basic relationship with Christ to stand the test when trials of your faith or death knock on the door of your life. One must never give up the fight in persevering to maintain the dignity of the priesthood or being a Christian when attacks or severe stress invade your life cycle . . . you must stand in the gap and fight the bullets! The contents of this writing are recorded to serve as documented and factual experience of one that has been there and done that! You can't tell a person about something that you don't know, nor can you take someone to a place that you haven't been! The record speaks for itself! You have but one life to live on this earth, so live it well, and love God and your neighbor!

(L-R) Chaplain Grooms and wife, Betty
at the Brigadier General Promotion Ceremony
Courtesy of SCMD/TAG

ACKNOWLEDGMENTS

When my wife, Betty, and I set out to do work in the ministry of our Lord over thirty-five years ago, we had no idea the day would come when we would be actively involved in an official military chaplaincy ministry that would carry us literally across the United States of America, and periodically, to foreign countries. But, God, knowing what our future would require, brought us together with many devoted and helpful friends. This unbelievable move of God allowed for a marvelous partnership with other talented, God-gifted individuals. It has given both of us the opportunity to become professionally-equipped partners, and we have been blessed beyond words to have been surrounded by equally dedicated Christian associates.

Laboring for the Lord has been a tireless journey for all of God's chosen few, only explainable by reason of devotion to Christ and His kingdom work. The chaplain ministry has grown gradually, and it continues to move progressively forward with a pattern of success that is only explained by the unusual gifts from our Heavenly Father to His servants.

To Him we give praise and honor!

INTRODUCTION

Come take a trip with me back in time. Our flashback experience will carry us across the pages of biblical and American military history. It will bring to light how important it is for a community to have clergy actively involved in their growth. A chaplain ministry sprang from the citizen clergy. It's a proven fact that clergy and chaplains are needed in every segment of society. Community organization is what the chaplaincy is all about, and what had to be faced by courageous men and women to provide compliance with the First Amendment of the U.S. Constitution.

We will review and take a hard look at what the call to chaplain service really requires of an individual when the test to stand for what's right represents itself.

We will reflect on biblical history, American military history and the community history surrounding the need to have clergy and chaplains.

We will identify the duties and responsibilities required of chaplains serving in the Army, Air Force, Coast Guard, and Marines, Navy, and National Guard as well as Reserves, CAP, state defense forces, et cetera.

An effort will be made to present the information in layman's language for the purpose of a more functional understanding of the role of a chaplain. Chaplain performance guidelines, military funeral, memorial and ceremonial procedures, military wedding and other related subjects will be targeted for special emphasis.

We will test the waters and explore the basics of the required performance of a chaplain, and examine the specific duties and responsibilities that go along with the chaplain ministry terrain. It will be a long, long trip, but I will try to be a good scout and navigator to those who will join me. It should be an interesting exploration for each person interested in the chaplaincy, and more gratifying to the individual who has an interest in reaching out to the military family from a religious vantage point. It should be fulfilling also to the person who believes in being faithful to the calling of God, loyalty to one's superior or commander, and most importantly . . . never, *never* having to compromise your religious faith.

But first let me, your traveling associate, make a confession. I have never written a book before, so I have to beg your indulgence and ask for your patience. However, my English and phrasing will be easy to read and follow. I promise to explain everything clearly and carefully as best I can. Also, it might be useful to add to this material your own personal research data. You will be able to glean from many sources, extracting data that will serve to eliminate the trial and error process you have experienced or you're presently going through. Having a probing, investigative and searching hunger to learn from others how best to perform as a chaplain will help you to be able to incorporate your own personal experience into the functional job description of what a chaplain must do to establish a workable approach. It is my personal objective, as you move closer to the end of your exploratory trip, that your time spent thus far will have been worth the pilgrimage.

There will be memories of individuals, families, subordinates, and superiors you have ministered to over the years. There is no turning back the time clock to adjust the manner in which you handled a situation or task. You will have left a mark on their lives in some form, and they will have left one on your life, also . . . nobody plans to do that . . . it just happens. The history of the experiences "we" had will be forever recorded in the pages of time. We will cherish the opportunity we had to serve; therefore, make good use of the time you have right now. Pick up the torch and make *your* mark as a chaplain! My papa once stated, "Good people come by every now and then, sorry ones are always with you." But, as chaplains, we will have to make an effort to rescue the perishing and care for the dying . . . winning some and losing some!

The Word of God prompts us: "Study to show thyself approved unto God." So . . . dig in and let's explore the past, observe the present and plan for the future! The base is built upon **faith**, **duty**, **honor** and **country** . . . serving God and loving America.

✟

Chapter One:

UNDERSTANDING THE CHAPLAIN AND THE MISSION

The Role of Clergy and their Mission at America's Beginning

From the very beginning of our nation it was almost as if people had an innate nature about them when it came to respecting the clergy. The minister represented to the community a direct connection to God, and when individuals experienced difficulties it seemed almost automatic to go to their minister for help. No wonder the church and the schoolhouse were among the first buildings to be constructed. They represented the ingredients, spiritual and educational, that communities and towns are made of. Even though some people were not churchgoers, neither were they well educated, it was an implied fact that God must have a place in every township, and must be a part of every person's life. This trend set the pace for respecting God, His Son and the Holy Spirit as a nation went to work making a way of life by realizing that God's help would make the difference . . . "In God We Trust!"

The role of the clergy and their mission at America's beginning is an underlying reason why America has been blessed with over 225 years of existence. An expressed declaration of faith and a belief in God were celebrated by a courageous group of people who had once lived in another country, and had had enough of their government's ridicule of its Christian people. This history is a reflection of a dream come true for our forefathers. They left behind the oppression, fear and outright discrimination in another country to set out, by faith, on a voyage to seek freedom and express their individuality in worshipping God. They learned early in their journey to put their *trust* and *faith* in God. And, their connection to God was the clergy.

The Bible became their guide. They identified themselves with the people of God characterized in the biblical story recorded in the Old Testament, the book of Exodus. Their expectations were backed up by their acceptance that the biblical word was true and factual. It was perhaps their belief that if the people in the biblical book of Exodus could find the promised land, and they did, then their journey to find a new nation, their promised land, would happen, too. And, it did happen.

One of the most encouraging and thrilling experiences, and no doubt a possible providential act of God, was an event in the history of those early settlers. It took place when they were about to reach the shoreline of what they believed to be their promised land.

Their intended destination was Plymouth Rock, but something miraculous happened, something that profoundly influenced the future of American life. It was a Saturday evening, and almost out of nowhere a severe storm came up before they could make land at Plymouth Rock. The storm on the sea drove them to make land on the shore of Clark Island. They disembarked and found a place of safety for the night on the island. The following morning, Sunday, the Godly character of those early settlers set in motion, as an example for all Christians to follow, a recognition and respect for God, especially on the Sabbath.

The next morning, instead of reloading their cargo on board their ship and continuing to sail toward Plymouth Rock, they spent the day in worship: praying, giving praise, and expressing a thankful heart for God's intervention in their lives. Their act of trust and faith in God expressed publicly a portrayal of a deep conviction about the Sabbath day. The success of their long voyage was realized on Monday, December 11, 1620; they landed at Plymouth Rock.

During the establishment of our new nation the early settlers from England included in their community development a show of respect for God by providing a place to worship, the church. This decision provided the basic groundwork needed for the organization of a church to function in the New World. The system utilized to call their first minister or priest to serve the congregation was to be an example for ages to come. Thus, being unaware of the significance it would have upon later generations, the role of the clergy and their mission were birthed in the newfound country. Religion was given a place in the early history of the nation called America. "In God we trust" was never more important! The dream of a new land came true, but that was just the beginning. Freedom, liberty and the pursuit of happiness, especially for Christians, had an expensive price tag.

God's representatives, the clergy, have been the people responsible for providing religious services to those interested in living a moral and productive lifestyle. The stability of any community is directly related to the religious faith of its inhabitants. Since the beginning of time, the human race, created by God and given the free moral agency to make decisions, have lacked the ability to make proper judgments. This weakness has caused much suffering that could have been avoided. The relationship between man and God was intended to exist with perfect harmony. It was not God's fault that a break in fellowship came about; it was the result of man's evildoing.

The unpredictable behavior of man created the need for periodic meetings with the clergy to make wrongs right in an approach to God through the minister! Counseling and deliverance were the necessary avenues used by the penitent man to make things right with God. Help was needed! Peace of mind was to be restored, and a return to the normal activities of life would hopefully continue once an individual established a meaningful relationship with God. In actuality, this created special work for the clergy, and took up a lot of their time. But, it paid great dividends.

Down through history the "representatives of God," the clergy, the pastor, the chaplain or whatever the label designated, have always been the human being's resource on earth to reach out for God's help and forgiveness. Their duties were recognized as honorable and trustworthy. Their availability to the people could be expected and depended upon. This type of dependency upon the clergy served to open the door for their representation of God in the palaces of kings and in the homes of ordinary men and women, and established the sanctuary, or church, as a place to be reconciled unto the Lord.

The clergy, and their priestly role, became a respected office. The duties and responsibilities of the clergy were defined in a specific manner, and were to be carried out beyond reproach.

The Old Testament Scriptures communicate to the clergy of today that the priest of the Bible was involved with people, not only to carry out priestly duties at the sanctuary, but also to possibly accompany soldiers to the battlefield. The priest must be available, flexible, and mobile in order to carry God's counsel and blessings to where the warriors gather.

When the priest is called upon to perform their Godly-ordained duties or to represent the office of the priest or clergy, the performance should be done in a professional manner. Liberal views *must* not change what is expected of a priest or clergyperson. Only those who are without sin should represent God, be it past, present or future. Men have redefined God's requirements for the priestly order. Sinful representation of God by ungodly clergy *must* not be condoned. Honorable clergy must stand together!

The duties of the priest have not changed too much over the centuries, but additional names for priests or clergy have been created due to the diversification of religious organizations. The labels, such as minister, clergy, Father, priest, pastor, evangelist, reverend and so forth, are given to identify the person as the Lord's representative. The labels and duties may have changed somewhat, but those who present themselves as representatives of God must be Godly individuals. And, believe it or not, those that purposely violate that trust will face the Lord for their sinful deeds. The calling to represent God is a sacred trust!

The early settler's leadership knew, without ever giving it a second thought, that security for their community was a priority. The establishment of a community militia was put into place. Volunteers were recruited, and out of that basic act America's first military "home guard" was birthed.

Leaders were appointed, a command structure was organized, and the duties and responsibilities were detailed and
outlined. This home guard military structure grew into a
ready force that eventually became the safeguard of every
community along the frontier, and later across the new
nation. Volunteerism was the backbone that prompted
George Washington to join the Virginia militia, and later to
gradually become actively involved in the military. Any
community is worth standing up for!

In 1620, our forefathers' primary reason behind coming
to a new country was for religious freedom; therefore, the
role of the priest or clergy took on a new dimension of service. Another field of labor for the priest or clergy grew out
of those efforts and was introduced to the church world in
1775. The title of "military chaplain" was added. Having
clergy serve as chaplains did *not* create the establishment of
a military religion; it became just another open door of
opportunity to represent God to soldiers at home or on the
battlefield. Military personnel *must* not be deprived of the
privilege and right to worship and express their religious
faith. The minister, priest, or pastor is the chaplain!

The ministry of the clergy and the church, reaching out
to people, should have the same goals. The title of a priest
or clergyperson, when performing in the military service, is
recognized as "chaplain." Chaplains have a heritage and
history of Godly service that reaches back in time, and by
the grace of God it will be carried forward with an even
greater service to mankind. Fighting the bullets of the
unethical behavior of the leadership made the chaplain the
prime target of those men. They did *not* want chaplains
around. The chaplain spoils the fun! He/she is a symbol representing Christ, and when the chaplain is out in the open,
they become a reminder of what "good" and "evil" are. The
record speaks for itself!

Thank God, the United States became the first nation to include the principles of religious freedom in its basic laws. This Freedom of Religion is understood to be the right of a person to form personal religious beliefs according to his or her own conscience and to give public expression to those beliefs in worship and teaching, restrictive only by the requirements of public order.

The chaplain is not permitted to bear arms, but he or she is armed with the Word of God, and that right is backed up by the United States Constitution and the First Amendment (Freedom of Religion, Press and Expression: "Congress shall make no laws respecting an establishment of religion, or prohibiting the free exercise thereof . . . "). The chaplain is a recognized spokesperson for God!

Ever since General George Washington made the decision to have clergy involved in the military, that very decision has caused many commanders, as well as other officers and NCO leadership, to secretly conspire to eliminate chaplains from their units. It really does not make sense that chaplains are given such a hard time. A few bad chaplains or clergy have created a lot of damage to the chaplaincy and the ministry, and unless a chaplain/clergy will monitor his or her own behavior, it will not get any better. Adultery, alcoholism, drug addiction, family abuse, homosexuality/gay activities, and many more behaviors common among men and women, have been the downfall of many talented chaplains/ministers. Sin has no respect for people. We must pray, and keep praying, for our chaplains/ministers.

However, until the full run of justice is taken to clear or convict an accused chaplain/minister, they will continue to get away with their criminal behavior, but not get away with their sinning, and leave a bad mark against all chaplains/ministers. Letting a chaplain/minister that is guilty escape the system, by allowing him or her just to resign, hurts to the core of the chaplaincy/ministry. From the spiritual side, the guilty chaplain/minister can repent and find grace in the eyes of God, and if we do not believe in forgiveness, we need to just close the church down. But, forgiveness is available for the repentant person. Repent because of Godly sorrow, not just because one gets caught! For all those found guilty: kick 'em out of active ministry as a chaplain/minister, report the action via their denomination process, and have the denomination make the final decision on their credentials. They have violated the sacred trust placed in them . . . slapping their hands is not the answer, removing them from the ministry should be the penalty! Leaving such bad chaplains/ministers in the ministry to counsel with others having the same problems is an outright injustice to the priesthood! Hard? Yes! The cause of God is bigger than any person or religious faith group! Fighting the bullets of sinfulness softened by liberals is the price to be paid by Godly men and women of the cloth! The fight is worth the battle! For those chaplains/ministers that have been found guilty of sinfulness during ministry service, and have repented and asked forgiveness, there are other places to serve in the chaplaincy/ministry outside of restoring them to their position as a chaplain or minister.

In the active military service when an individual performs terribly and not responsibly repeatedly, a discharge labeled "undesirable" is processed after being found guilty and out he/she goes! The minister in civilian life who fits this category should be dismissed in the same manner as a chaplain is found guilty. Clergypersons must be responsible for their behavior at all times or suffer the consequences of dismissal for serious offenses, and not be allowed to enter the ministry as a minister under any circumstance.

✝

Chapter Two:

THE CHAPLAIN REFLECTED IN BIBLICAL HISTORY

Man's inability to control himself or his emotions, or to establish a relationship with his creator, has been seen repeatedly throughout human history. Tracing man's evolution, either through the theory of evolution, or through the belief in the biblical creation account, has created a difficult decision path for some people. But, I have no problem believing in the Bible!

Therefore, to give man the help that he so desperately needed to maintain a relationship with God, the office of priest was instituted. Man now would have help in reconciling himself to God when sinful deeds were done.

The unpredictable behavior of man created the need for periodic meetings with the priest to make wrongs right in an approach to God through the priest! The penitent man experienced counseling and deliverance. Peace of mind was to be restored, and a return to the normal activities of life would occur. In actuality, this created special work for the priest, and took up a lot of his time.

The relationship between God and man, especially the priest, makes it important for me to place great emphasis again on the fact that down through history the priest has always been God's representative before man. His duties were recognized as honorable and trustworthy. His availability to the people could be expected and depended upon. This type of dependency upon the priest served to open the door for the representation of God in the palaces of kings, and in the homes of ordinary men and women, and established the sanctuary as a place to be reconciled unto God. The priest and his priestly role became a respected office. The duties and responsibilities of the priest were defined in a specific manner, and were to be carried out beyond reproach.

The Old Testament Scriptures communicate to the clergy of today that the priest was involved with people, not only to carry out priestly duties at the sanctuary, but called upon to accompany soldiers to the battlefield. The priest or clergy must be flexible and mobile to carry God's counsel and blessings to where the warriors gather.

Biblical References
The Priest at Work

The chaplaincy has an honored tradition that has been passed down through the history of the United States of America. Chaplains of all religious faiths have provided ministry to our military personnel, both enlisted men and officers. In providing a religious ministry and presenting it to military personnel, chaplains of past history have always had to deal with difficult assignments that will forever be encountered by the clergy of all religious faiths. Whether in time of peace or in time of war, chaplains have helped service personnel find the strength that only God could give. The efforts put forth by chaplains, and supported by many commanders, have provided the perseverance needed to continue the fight to maintain the chaplaincy service for the military personnel.

There is no better source than the Bible to rightly focus in on where priests or chaplains fit in when battle is being waged and duties and responsibilities are being put into action. As we search the records, we may be convinced by the facts that the priest or chaplain is needed to shepherd the military flock during good times as well as in war or distressful times.

The chaplain is, primarily because of the position, a counselor on religious affairs to the commander and his staff. Fighting to have one's religious faith respected, compounded by actual war situations, perhaps pre-dates recorded history. God has always honored nations that put their trust in Him. The historical record of the Israelites, dating back to approximately 2000 B.C., had religious leaders ministering to the established military personnel. The facts are sufficiently documented in Deuteronomy.

Deuteronomy 20:1-4:
> When you go forth to war against your enemies, and see horses and chariots and an army larger than your own, you shall not be afraid of them; for the Lord your God is with you, who brought you up out of the land of Egypt. And when you draw near the battle, the priest shall approach and speak unto the people, And shall say unto them, "Hear O Israel, ye approach this day unto battle against your enemies: let not your hearts faint, fear not, and do not tremble, neither be ye terrified because of them; For the Lord your God is He that goes with you, to fight for you against your enemies, to give you victory.

The priests would accompany the Hebrew army to the battlefield and would involve themselves by leading in worship, and encouraging all personnel. During this time in ancient history, it was simple for the priest to do that, and very logical because Israel operated under a theocratic government.

Also, even the Greek and Roman armies would practice and beseech "divine" help in time of battle, make condemnations of blame against their enemies, and do it through ceremonies and prayers. It served to reinforce morale. The priests would accompany the troops to the battle scene and participate, as instructed by their leader.

Another Scripture reference is recorded in Joshua 6:5-6, where General Joshua had the priests actively involved during the successful taking of Jericho. They performed important functions, and were allowed to be at the orientation when the battle plan strategy was communicated to commanders.

Joshua 6:5-6:

> And it shall come to pass, that when they make a long blast with the rams' horn; and when ye hear the sound of the trumpet, all the people shall shout with a great shout; and the wall of the city shall fall down flat, and the people shall ascend up every man straight before him. And Joshua the son of Nun called the priests, and said unto them, "Take up the Ark of the Covenant, and let seven priests bear seven trumpets of rams' horns before the ark of the Lord."

General Joshua had faith in the priests and their Godly ability to be supportive to his leadership in winning the battle over the enemy. He did not hesitate having the priests at the scene of battle nor did he have second thoughts about involving the priests, especially as participants. The priest or chaplain is the advisor to the commander on religious affairs. The priest or chaplain *must* be loyal to his commander, and perform the chaplain duties and other assigned responsibilities without reservation. Therefore, it enhances the strength of the commander to utilize his priest or chaplain, and it makes good sense when it also makes an positive impression upon the troops. It communicates faith in God and sends a message to the troops that teamwork, loyalty and respect work!

Events of Significant Consequence
Conversion of Constantine

The conversion of Constantine, the fourth century Roman emperor, was indirectly influenced by a Christian witness that brought before him the opportunity to know God, and earn His respect. It initiated a change in Constantine's life, and opened the door for a greater witness. Christianity was adopted by the Roman empire.[1] Some believe, and I am among that number, that it was the inside work of a chaplain-type priest taking advantage of the opportunity to recommend to the emperor that he give God a chance to work with him as a leader, and among the people as well. The acceptance was witnessed, and it surely helped!

Council of Ratisbon

During the Middle Ages, the Roman Catholic Church, recognized the chaplaincy as a valuable asset. The chaplaincy representation and its mission were officially recognized in 742 A.D. by the Council of Ratisbon. The council prohibited the chaplain (the servant of God) in every way from bearing arms or fighting in the army or going against the enemy, except those alone who because of the sacred office, namely for the celebrating of mass and caring for the relics of the saints, have been designated for the office; that is to say, the leader may have with him one or two bishops with their priest chaplains, and each captain may have one priest, in order to hear the confessions of the men and impose upon them the proper penance.

This proved to be a vital precedent establishing chaplains as non-combatants, and was formalized 1100 years later, for the modern world, in the Geneva Convention of 1864.[2]

Saint Martin of Tours

The research of chaplaincy goes back in history and connects itself to the legend of Saint Martin of Tours. He was a fourth century Roman soldier on his way to a battle scene. As he traveled along the way he met a shivering beggar beside the road. He had nothing to share with the beggar in need, except his own cloak. Martin, without hesitation, disrobed himself and divided the cloak with his sword, wrapped it around the man, and continued on his journey to the duty station. It was an experience he could not forget. That night, according to legend, Martin had a vision in which he saw Christ wearing the half-cloak he had shared with the beggar.

As a result of what he saw in his dream and the impression it had on his life, Martin was converted to Christianity. The story circulated far and wide. The remnant of Martin's cloak was given to a priest. The priest placed it in a safe depository and kept it as a memorial to Martin. The story reached the ears of the king of France. He became so enlightened over the spiritual significance of the divided cloak that he declared it a sacred garment. It became a sacred relic taken into battle by French kings.

Martin completed his military obligation, and later devoted his life to the church. His influence over others placed him in a special category, and after his death Martin of Tours became the patron saint of France.

In Latin, the cloak was called the *cappa*. Its portable shrine was called the *capella* and its caretaker priest, the *cappellanus*.

Eventually, all clergy affiliated with the military were called *capellani*, or, in French, called *chapelains*. The term now applies to representatives of all distinctive faith groups in the military. This provided a springboard for the future creativity of the mission of the chaplaincy.[3]

✝

Chapter Three:

REFLECTING ON AMERICAN HISTORY

Every community's base strength, no matter how small or how large the population happens to be, was established on a religious faith in God. Every individual, during peace-time or wartime, *must* be given the opportunity to practice their religious faith, and be afforded the opportunity to express their belief in God. That's what freedom was all about! The quest for religious freedom prompted the pil-grims to leave England in search of a country where they could live as free people, and have religious freedom to express their faith in God without reprisals.

This search had its beginning in 1620 and it continued through the early 1700s. Churches sprung up in every com-munity. Clergy of many faith groups became involved in community development, and where the church was involved, the community was strong. No matter where good is being done, bad will surface its ugly face, and try to destroy. It was no different with the early Americans; war became commonplace in the fight for freedom. Therefore, established communities have always had to share their most prized possessions, their citizens. The fight for free-dom claimed many young men and clergy, too. Yes, the community clergy stepped forward and volunteered their services, when needed.

It is an understandable fact that war brings death. Death and illness know no boundary. It does not recognize peace or war. It invades one's life at the least expected time. Therefore, the soldier must be allowed the opportunity to have a member of the clergy nearby when unexpected problems occur, even death or serious illness. The prayers and the visible presence of the clergy were welcomed in yesteryear, and continue to be welcomed today. Clergy are valuable assets for a community in times of peace and war. During the first year of the war in 1775, clergy would step forward to become involved as nonmilitary members of the Army. But, later this changed for the better; the military clergy position was officially titled chaplain. Their initial pay was twenty dollars each month.

The respect and recognized need for chaplains had its greatest day when a small group of volunteer clergy, fifteen in number, stood proudly in the ranks of the first formation assembly by General George Washington when he took command of the Continental Army near Cambridge, Massachusetts on July 3, 1775. Washington could not help but take notice of the fifteen clergy as they joined themselves together with 14,000 soldiers on that historic day for clergy/chaplains. When the breakdown of his regiments was reported to him, Washington realized the number of clergy was insufficient to meet the spiritual needs of his troops. His concern for his soldiers' religious welfare prompted him to give priority to staffing more clergy. Therefore, he prepared his official requisition report for food, clothing, powder, blankets and other items, and presented it to the Continental Congress. At the top of the list was an urgent request to consider the clergy for needed chaplain positions. Convincing the higher authorities of the importance of having clergy represented in the military command was not an easy task for Washington. But, his overpowering reasoning was respected; he won out. It was his personal persistence and carefully planned actions that prompted the Continental Congress, on July 29, 1775, to officially approve the Army chaplain positions.

The "birthday" of the military chaplaincy is recognized on July 29, 1775. Another step of progress for the Army chaplain occurred almost two years later. In May 1777, the Continental Congress, again under the official request from Washington, approved additional assignments for chaplains as brigade chaplains.

Almost to the day, a year later in May 1778 at Valley Forge, the commander in chief, General Washington, took another step in support of the duties of the chaplains. He issued an order that religious services would be conducted on Sunday, and officers and noncommissioned officers would set an example by their attendance. This action was not very popular, but nevertheless, it was the beginning of the beginning for approved religious services.

Therefore, to honor General George Washington's effort and to express appreciation on behalf of chaplains, his life story, in abbreviated form, is included in this manuscript. He played a major role in bringing chaplains into the military family. All military men and women of every branch of service have benefited from his conviction that religious rights of all soldiers everywhere must not be ignored!

Honor and Tribute to General George Washington

Chaplains serving in the armed forces of the United States of America, past, present and future, owe a debt of gratitude to General George Washington. He was instrumental in:

- getting chaplains recognized and respected as chaplains;

- getting chaplains commissioned as military officers;
- having chaplains placed on the Army payroll;
- establishing and approving worship service locations;
- personally encouraging both enlisted men and officers to attend religious services; and
- establishing the need for chaplains throughout the Continental Army.

There were fights with some Army brass in backroom conferences over the subject of having chaplains; these often took up a lot of Washington's time. Washington led the fight because he believed it was worth the effort. The Army, especially Washington, needed chaplains to be on the military team. Chaplains' acceptance as a part of the military by the leadership was proven by Washington to be an ingredient that helped morale, and definitely did not hurt his command.

There are still military commanders of our present generation just as interested in having chaplains on staff as Washington was. They, too, have to fight to keep chaplains equally represented in the military. They value and respect the office of the chaplain and the part they play in accomplishing their mission.

For someone to oppose having chaplains in the military reveals the lack of knowledge and respect for the Constitution of the United States and First Amendment rights. The Army Chaplaincy was found to be Constitutional under the First Amendment. " . . . Congress shall make no laws respecting an establishment of religion, nor prohibiting the free exercise thereof." Thus, the first order of priority for military chaplains, Constitutionally speaking, is to assist all military people who desire such assistance to practice their faith as deemed militarily practical. Wherever the military stations or assigns military personnel, a chaplain *must* be available to give religious support to all of the troops when needed.

In essence, what the First Amendment is implying to the military is that after bringing men and women into the military service from all walks of life, all religious faiths and backgrounds, training them, mobilizing and deploying them around the world, often to remote locations where they are sometimes placed in harm's way, do not deprive *any* military personnel from having access to a chaplain. It's a small price to pay for the spiritual welfare of the men and women in uniform and their families.

General George Washington

George Washington was born in Westmoreland County, Virginia on February 22, 1732. He was the oldest son of Augustine Washington and his second wife, Mary Bell Washington. His early life was spent at the family estate on Pope's Creek along the Potomac River. In school, he studied the regular subjects of reading, writing and arithmetic, but his main interest in the surveyor trade won out. He was able to get a job as a surveyor and helped lay out the town of Belhaven, Virginia (now known as Alexander). Washington's father died in 1743, and soon after the burial of his father, he lived with his half brother Lawrence at Mount Vernon. Lawrence became a substitute father-type to George, and treated him like he was a son. However, nine years later, Lawrence came down with tuberculosis and died. Washington ultimately inherited the Mount Vernon estate.

In addition to the many farming duties required of Washington to keep Mount Vernon productive, he squeezed in a little time to follow up on his personal interest in the military activities of the home guard. He saw this involvement as a means to provide the community with a military force, if and when needed. But, it also gave Washington an opportunity to become involved in the military on a limited basis. His commitment to having a military home guard, and to having the necessary training completed, was soon recognized by his superiors.

This opened the door for him to be appointed as one of the four military adjutants primarily responsible for military training in Virginia. He was commissioned as a major in the Virginia militia. His interest in the military and having a trained, ready force motivated Washington toward becoming an active duty soldier. Within a year, he volunteered for active duty.[4]

Military Life

In 1753, a disagreement between the British and the French over control of the Ohio Valley erupted into a full-scale war known as the French and Indian War (1754-63). This war created a need for experienced, military-trained soldiers. It provided an opportunity, not only for Washington, but also for all home guard-trained young men having a desire to join the active duty military. Washington volunteered for active duty, and was commissioned at the rank of major.

Washington did not have to wait long before being assigned a command. He and his troops were dispatched on a mission to warn the French commander at Fort Le Boeuf against further infringement on the territory presently occupied by the British. The dangers and difficulties Washington and his troops encountered in accomplishing the mission were described in detail in a written report submitted to his commander.

Washington's commander reported to his own superior that even though Washington was young and inexperienced, his previous military training provided the necessary ingredients needed to be selected for the mission he was assigned. His performance and early success as a leader earned Washington the respect of his superiors, and for his outstanding service he was promoted to lieutenant colonel at the age of twenty-two. The promotion to lieutenant colonel prompted Washington to place priority on studying military tactics of other successful and more experienced officers. He did not hesitate to seek advice from the other experienced senior officers in his command. His popularity and respect among his troops and other officers gave Washington the confidence he needed to excel in military circles.[5]

Washington's Military Experiences

Washington was assigned to another troop command and ordered to establish a post at the Forks of the Ohio (present-day Pittsburgh). His command was severely tested and overwhelmed by the French in a daylong battle fought during a steady, hard rain. His command was greatly outnumbered and surrounded by the enemy. His food supply was almost exhausted. His dampened ammunition was almost useless, and his command would surely be wiped out in a matter of time. After much soul searching, Washington was forced to negotiate surrender to the better-equipped and stronger enemy force. Under the terms of the surrender, Washington was permitted to have his command lay down their arms and march back to Williamsburg. The surrender of all arms was done without incident, resulting in the command's safe departure from the area and their safe return to their own lines.[6]

Washington Resigns His Commission

Discouraged by his defeat in battle, and the memory of having to surrender his command to the enemy, compounded by discrimination between the British and colonial officers over pay and rank, Washington resigned his commission and returned to Mount Vernon near the end of 1754.[7]

Washington Returns to the Army

In 1755, Washington joined Major General Edward Braddock as his aide and was given the courtesy rank of colonel. A short time later Braddock gave him a troop command and within a few weeks he became involved in a battle against the French. General Braddock and his command were ambushed by the French and Indian allies. During the battle, Washington's display of courage, tactical skills and heroic efforts were recognized. His military reputation spread like wildfire.

Washington was rewarded by his superiors for his outstanding leadership. He was promoted to colonel (at age 23), and appointed commander in chief of the Virginia militia with specific orders to defend the colony's frontier.

Washington was seen by his superiors as having evolved from a bold, egotistical, and assertive young officer, intolerant with restraints and given to writing admonishing letters to his superiors, to a mature soldier with a grasp of administration and a firm understanding of how to deal effectively with civilian authority. However, in early 1759, Washington became irritated with the government's failure to supply the soldiers adequately, coupled with the slow process of promotion; he resigned and returned home to Mount Vernon. Washington was convinced that the frontier was safe from French assault. He left the Army and returned to Mount Vernon, giving priority to restoring his neglected estate.

In the spring of 1759, he married Martha Dandridge Curtis, a wealthy widow with two children. They returned to Mount Vernon and began a restoration of the home place. His many influential friends convinced Washington to enter politics and run for a seat in the Virginia House of Burgesses. He followed their advice, and ran for the office. He won the election to the House of Burgesses and served from 1759 to 1774 as a Whig leader.[8]

Washington Returns to the Army Again

In June, 1775, after the Lexington and Concord bloodshed against the British, Congress appointed Washington as Commander in Chief of the Continental Army with the rank of general. The fight with the British was no easy job. Washington took command of the troops surrounding British-occupied Boston at Cambridge, Massachusetts on July 3, 1775. He found the command of twenty-three regiments, consisting of 14,000 soldiers, badly in need of tactical training, a restoration of discipline, and a morale boost.

After a further review of his command, he became aware that he only had fifteen volunteer clergy on staff. He realized from previous experience that there was value in having clergy to serve as part of his command. At this time, especially, he needed all the support he could muster, including the clergy, to bring his command up to fighting capabilities. Therefore, he immediately gave priority to recognizing the clergy as part of the Army; he gave them the designated name of "chaplain." He met with them and asked for their assistance in recruiting other clergy into the military. The recruitment resulted in an increased number of clergy who patriotically volunteered to serve. This unbelievable support by the chaplains prompted Washington to put together a promotional plan of action to convince the Continental Congress that all soldiers deserved to have access to a chaplain for religious purposes. His efforts were very successful. It paved the way for the Continental

Congress to approve his chaplain recommendations, and passed into law the establishment of a chaplain staff for the Army.[9]

Chaplains Approved and Staffed in the Army by the Continental Congress (July 29, 1775)

The chaplain recommendations by Washington set in motion the action taken by the Continental Congress in approving chaplains for the Army. On July 29, 1775 the Continental Congress officially established the Army chaplaincy. This date will forever be known as the birthday of the chaplaincy.

The official establishment of the Army chaplaincy included the creation of a pay scale for chaplains: CH-20. This act was interpreted to mean that chaplains would be paid on the same pay scale as a captain—twenty dollars monthly. Later, the chaplain pay was increased to thirty-three dollars monthly, the same pay scale as a colonel. This action was the first official recognition of chaplains by the American government.

In addition to working on the establishment of an official chaplaincy branch for the Army, Washington took an immediate hands-on command approach, and initiated a restoration training cycle to get his command in tiptop shape to fight. It took two months to bring his command around to a satisfied state of readiness. He utilized his chaplains to assist in accomplishing this task.

Washington's firm leadership, charisma, devotion to the cause, complete trust in God, extraordinary leadership skills, and command experience contributed greatly in gaining the respect, hearts, and loyalty of his officers and troops. In the dark days before him, Washington reaped the benefits of his Godly wisdom in having the support of his chaplains. He was a man of Christian character, and made it a habit to pray daily for the Lord's spiritual guidance. This proved to be one of the strongest elements that carried him through the difficult times in his military career.

Almost two years after the official establishment of the chaplaincy, in May 1777, the chaplain branch of the Army progressed to another milestone; chaplains were officially assigned to perform duties and responsibilities as brigade chaplains.

Again, almost one year later, on May 2, 1778, at Valley Forge, General Washington so highly valued chaplains that he gave the general order to include in the Army recruitment program the official recruitment of chaplains. Standards were drafted to recruit the clergy. They were to be persons of good character, having lived exemplary lives as clergy, and were required to have the recommendations of their religious faith group. His order communicated the chaplain recruitment standards and included the following:

The commander in chief directed that every officer and enlisted soldier will:
- pay the chaplain suitable respect;
- perform religious services every Sunday at eleven o'clock at a designated location in each brigade having an assigned chaplain, and the brigades that have no chaplains assigned will attend religious services at places of worship nearest them;
- furthermore, it is expected that officers of all ranks will, by their attendance, set an example.

The ministry of the chaplain was widely accepted once General Washington issued his order directly requiring that officers and enlisted personnel recognize the office of the chaplain and give immediate respect. It was this historic act of recognition and respect for the chaplain that established the base from which chaplains could provide members of the armed forces of the United States with spiritual guidance, pastoral care, moral support and morale leadership. The chaplain serves his commander as "chief advisor on matters pertaining to the religious care of the Army."[10]

War Ends on October 19, 1781

In 1780, the main theater of war shifted to the south. Washington's general staff officers consisted of outstanding men such as Benedict Arnold, Horatio Gates, Nathaniel Greene, and Daniel Morgan, to name a few. After the arrival of the French army in 1780, Washington concentrated on coordinating joint allied efforts to guarantee peaceful terms, and in 1781 launched the brilliantly-planned and executed Yorktown campaign again Charles Cornwallis, securing an American victory. The war ended on October 19, 1781.

Word of Washington's reputation and fighting spirit spread extremely fast during the war. He demonstrated his military genius and skill in the defeat of the British. He was a commander that believed in God and demonstrated his faith by living a Godly life. He believed in training his troops and demanded that they be disciplined to perform adequately in battle, and he would take every step possible in supplying them with what was needed to wage war. He was known as a commander with integrity, as a commander with intelligence, as a commander with energy, and as a commander that had publicly expressed his faith in God. A respected leader!

Washington was once again facing retirement as Commander in Chief of the Continental Army. He was again returning to Mount Vernon to be with his wife and live out his well-earned retirement on the banks of the Potomac. He did not anticipate that his retirement would be short-lived. He always felt that the Lord was using him in a special way, and the Creator would have the last word by issuing him his final retirement orders.

Washington, a man of unquestionable character, lived his life by principles that most men failed to value. He began his military career by accepting the advice of more experienced officers, and always progressed at a fast pace. Every day was a personal challenge for him to do his best for God and country. He quickly learned through many experiences throughout his military life to trust God's leading, and have faith in his own judgment. This was what ultimately made the young soldier become a man.

Success followed his flag. After many battle plans were finalized, and many victories were won, the war that ended on October 19, 1781 was an American triumph, not only for him but also for the country.

After the war, Washington returned to Mount Vernon. He kept a low profile but involved himself in periodic meetings with other war veterans. This affiliation with veterans resulted in his election as president of the Society of the Cincinnati, an organization of former Revolutionary War officers. He avoided Virginia politics so he could get his home place back in order again. But, he always kept up with the latest news!¹¹

Political Career: U.S. President

In May 1787, Washington attended the Virginia delegation to the Continental Convention in Philadelphia and was unanimously elected presiding officer. After the new Constitution was submitted to the states for ratification in 1788 and it became legally operative, he was unanimously chosen by the electoral college as the first president of the United States in 1789.

Washington took office and was sworn in on April 30, 1789 in New York City. He acted carefully and deliberately, being aware of the need to build an executive structure that could accommodate future presidents in keeping the office of the president strong and protected.

He gave God the credit for inspiring and impressing upon him the urgency to put into a written record the duties and responsibilities that guided him as he performed his duties as president. The future of America would forever benefit from his divinely-inspired structuring of the governmental duties of elected officials. His serious side and personal interest in America, and how she would grow, have provided the basic government structure to move progressively forward.[12]

Washington Elected for a Second Term

He was reelected in 1792. He accepted his second term so that he could complete the work he started when elected for his first term. However, when his second term was nearing an end, he considered all alternatives and, after much prayer, refused to run for a third term. After his presidency was over, Washington gracefully went home to Mount Vernon believing his work as president was complete.

By March 1797, when Washington left office, the country's financial system was well established, the Indian threat east of the Mississippi had been largely eliminated, and his successor, federalist vice-president John Adams, could pick up the reins of leadership.

Washington's experience, respect for the military, and unofficial counsel were needed to keep and maintain a strong Army force. He was asked to serve again as the Commander in Chief of the Continental Army. Although Washington reluctantly accepted command of the Army in

1798, he did so at a time when war with France seemed imminent. His services were needed, but the mere news of his return was enough to strike fear in the French government. His services were not used. He was always willing to put his country ahead of his own interests.

As Commander in Chief of the Army, Washington did not assume an active role. He instituted a "delegated" command style more out of convenience than need. This style involved Washington delegating duties and responsibilities to his general staff. This system proved to be a testing ground for future command staff. The command style he utilized was his way of combining both styles, "delegate" and "participatory," into a functioning command. It was a command style that functioned by delegating specific responsibilities to trusted and capable senior staff officers to get the job done. It worked very well and distributed his workload among future military commanders.[13]

Washington's Final Retirement

Washington preferred to spend his last years in happy retirement. On December 12, 1799, he began his last actual workday around Mount Vernon. Late in the afternoon of the same day he became very sick, came down with a high fever and could hardly whisper a word.

Throughout the night he continued to have difficulty swallowing and breathing due to severe pain in his throat area. The next morning his condition grew worse. His wife sent for the doctor. The doctor came right away. The diagnosis of Washington's illness was checked and evaluated by three different doctors. Each of them came up with the same opinion: his symptoms were caused by acute laryngitis. The doctors exhausted all possible methods of medical treatment. His condition continued to get worse, and was upgraded to critical. His health declined rapidly over the next twenty-four hours. Washington, age sixty-seven, died at his homeplace of Mount Vernon at 10:20 P.M. the night of December 14, 1799. The cause of death: acute laryngitis. He was buried at Mount Vernon on December 18, 1799 at 3:00 P.M. In his will, he set all of his slaves free.

Government officials wanted to bury him in a vault placed under the Capitol. While Washington was still living, the subject of his burial came up. His political friends explained to him they wanted to honor him at death by placing him in a vault under the Capitol. Under pressure from his friends, he agreed for that to be done. The burial place was built, but the family decided to honor what they understood to be Washington's personal request to be buried at Mount Vernon. The burial place and vault under the Capitol remains to this day, but George Washington is not buried there.

Washington's Military Funeral

Washington was the first government leader to be buried with full military honors. It is ironic that a chaplain assisted with the planning and conducting of the funeral. The last honor, respect, and tribute to be bestowed upon a veteran is the military funeral. Chaplains everywhere, of all branches of military service, will forever remember General George Washington as the commander who fought the Continental Congress for the right to have chaplains officially become a part of the military force.[14]

✝

Chapter Four:

LEGALISM: CIVILIAN AND MILITARY

The title, position or office, be it civilian or military, known as chaplain, is commonly understood and believed to be held by a clergy member or ministerial person. Also, within that same framework, one would furthermore have the understanding that the person would have and hold ministerial credentials with a recognized religious faith group. In addition, the individual would have verifiable ecclesiastical endorsement, ministerial experience, and an educational and training background.

It is assumed to be a fact that when a chaplain position or title is designated upon an individual, that person represents almighty God, and the person should conduct the heavenly Father's business by following a code of ethics. *True statement!* No other title carries with it such Godly responsibility as does the designation of chaplain or clergy. Many individuals possibly think of the chaplaincy as just another religious faith, and classify it as a civic or military religion. However, that is far from the truth, as far away as North is from South!

However, in most cases when an individual serves as a chaplain in civilian-life organizations, their credentials are not reviewed and verified as compared to the manner which the military requires. But, if the person is applying for a paid chaplain position in the business world, the qualifications are somewhat the same as required by the military. The statement is best expressed by a U.S. Marine Corps advertisement, "We need a few good men." There is a need for God-called men and women to serve as volunteer and paid chaplains in the community, and as members of a military branch of service.

The individual desiring to become a chaplain or clergyperson must have faith in God, and back that faith up with obedient behavior to the commandments of God. Down through history, men of all walks of life have fallen from God's grace because of sinful behavior. However, repentance is the way to be restored to God's favor. If the clergy and the congregation does not believe that willful sinning will sever the relationship one has with God, and that the person committing the sin can be forgiven by God, and afterwards be restored to His grace, then the doors of the sanctuary, church or chapel need to be closed. An individual can be restored to God's grace by way of Godly sorrow! Whatever the sins may have been, or presently are, in the life of an individual, God will forgive. It is suspected that there are many clergy or chaplains practicing ungodly homosexual and lesbian behaviors. Those individuals caught up in this deviant behavior lay claim to the theory that such behavior is inborn, but it is not. It is a learned behavior. Homosexual and lesbian behaviors are sinful acts, regardless of who the individuals are that commit or practice them. Persons committing those sinful acts can be forgiven by God, and restored to His grace. But, *no* chaplain should be ordained or permitted to become a chaplain while he or she practices homosexuality or lesbianism. There is no reason to continue to comment on this area of immorality.

Consequently, no God-called clergy can get involved in this deviant behavior and hide behind the cloth without knowing that it is wrong. I would dare to say, we have some hiding behind this veil of impersonation. If a chaplain or clergyperson is gay, then they should come forth and proclaim it publicly. They should not hide out of fear. If the person claiming to be gay believes there is no wrong in practicing that behavior, or that it is not sinful, why deny it? They should not lie about it. Also, if one believes that the gay lifestyle is righteous living, then they should be truthful to themselves, and not continue to live a lie! Come forth!

Individuals desiring to become a chaplain can explore opportunities in the active duty military (Army, Air Force, Coast Guard and Navy). Also, there are opportunities for chaplain reserve duty service in Army, Air Force, and Navy commands, and in the Army and Air National Guards.

In addition, there are opportunities for volunteer chaplains in some states that have reenacted state laws to reorganize and put back in force, under the command of the state's adjutant general, the military reserve manpower referred to in colonial days as the "state militia." In some states the name "militia" has been changed to State Guard, State Defense Force, State Reserve, et cetera. The organizational structure, duties, responsibilities and training are specifically outlined by the adjutant general. The utilization of this special military reserve manpower, subject to call-up by the adjutant general (TAG) in times of emergency or disaster, falls into the category of a trained military backup to be assigned to tasks within the state at a considerable savings to the taxpayer. There are no requirements for military duty to be served outside of the state.

United States Constitution

The preamble of the United States Constitution states emphatically that all men have rights, and that the government is to make sure those rights are secure. . . .

> We the People of the United States, in Order to form a more perfect Union, establish Justice, insure domestic Tranquility, provide for the common defence, promote the general Welfare, and secure the Blessings of Liberty to ourselves and our Posterity, do ordain and establish this Constitution for the United States of America.[15]

The First Amendment

The First Amendment, insuring freedom of religion, press and expression, states:

> Congress shall make no law respecting an establishment of religion, or prohibiting the free exercise thereof; or abridging the freedom of speech, or of the press; or the right of the people peaceably to assemble, and to petition the Government for a redress of grievances.

The U.S. Code, Title 10, Sections 3073, 3547 and 3581, establishes the position of the chaplain. It also describes the duties of chaplains, and requires commanders to provide for the religious needs of the military personnel and their families. On December 28, 1909, the War Department established the position of "chaplain assistant" in General Orders #253. Chaplains have chaplain assistants to help promote and carry out the religious program of the commands.[16]

Legal Issues: U.S. Code, Title 10
Separation of Church and State

The legal issues relating to chaplains and the law, including separation of church and state, are very important. They are vital to a complete understanding of the issue. To arrive at some understanding and get a truly worthwhile concept of the issue, you only have to go back to July 29, 1775, when the Continental Congress authorized chaplains to be a part of the military, and established the pay for chaplains. This historic action and recognition occurred before the signing of the Declaration of Independence.

It must be clearly understood by chaplains of all religious faiths that the authorization of chaplain positions does not imply the establishment of a military religion. Every chaplain must have their ministerial credentials from a recognized religious faith group, and be given endorsement by them to provide professional ministry in the selected military branch of service. It must be clearly understood that the chaplain remains fully accountable to their religious faith group authority. In so doing, the chaplain serves as that religious faith group's representative and not as a representative of a military religion.

The United States Code, Title 10, formally establishes the authorization of chaplains to serve in the armed forces. It also defines the legal parameters of the chaplaincy. Various legal decisions regarding historic and modern day challenges to the constitutionality of the chaplaincy have upheld the constitutional validity and legal necessity of the military chaplaincy.

The phrase "separation of church and state" has always threatened the freedom of the religious rights of individuals, and represents a built-in divisive framework for understanding how religion and government are related when these different institutions make formal claims within the same society.

The United States, as a new nation, undertook what was intended to be the protection of the religious rights of all its citizens. An important concept in the early history of the United States was the agreement that the federal government should recognize the religious freedom of individuals. The Bill of Rights draws a line between church and government, rather than erecting a wall of separation between church and state.

The religious rights of all people, civilian or military, must be guaranteed by the represented authority. That authority must be held accountable for its decisions. Thus, the chaplain can, without fear of being reprimanded for promoting the religious rights of military personnel, provide spiritual chaplain leadership. Nowhere but in America can religious rights be protected!

However, the chaplain must be loyal to the commander, loyal to the religious faith group represented and loyal to the men and women dependent upon the chaplain ministry support. There will be times when the chaplain will find himself standing alone against unethical practices of superiors, subordinates and others.

A few examples will be reflected upon at a later time.

✝

Chapter Five:

CHAPLAIN QUALIFICATIONS

Specific Functional Chaplain Roles

The chaplaincy ministry is a special ministry that is set apart from most descriptive ministerial categories of religious service. The roles of the chaplain are specific, functional, and ever-changing. The *American Heritage Dictionary* defines "specific" as precise, and "functional" as well-designed. "Chaplain" is defined as a clergyperson attached to a chapel who conducts religious services for a legislative assembly; or a clergyman attached to a military unit. Therefore, it does not take a rocket scientist to realize the value in having a chaplain on staff . . . a person with a message of hope, redemption, deliverance and spiritual support.

It is from these basic definitions that I launch out into familiar sacred territory. However, I must right away ask for your permission to personally change the word "clergyman" to read "clergyperson." The reasoning behind this action is to respect the call of clergypersons, male or female. God does the calling; individuals, male or female, do the answering to that call. In some denominational circles, they do not ordain or license females as clergypersons. This may be understood, yet not totally acceptable by other denominations or clergy. God calls "individuals"; denominations don't have that same authority. A God-called individual truly answering the call for service as a chaplain knows the burden has been lifted once the hurdles of obedience and acceptance are cleared. Nobody has the authority to call a person to become a chaplain; this phase of one's ministry must come from and through Almighty God.

Chaplain Role
Civilian Environment

Civic organizations, correctional facilities, hospitals, law enforcement agencies and veteran organizations have volunteers serving as chaplains, and they independently set up their own criteria of selection. In civic-type organizations, when a chaplain is appointed or elected to perform, the duties and responsibilities of that office usually consist of just praying. In addition, if the chaplain performs chaplain duties and responsibilities in correctional facilities, hospitals, law enforcement agencies and nursing homes, the ministerial duties will probably be done in the same manner as a pastor would do them. However, if the chaplain is to become a paid staff member, there will be a formal list of qualifications to meet via an application and interview process before actually being hired. It is recommended that the applicant hired to perform as a chaplain should meet the same basic qualifications required of a military chaplain (ministerial experience, education and ecclesiastical endorsement).

Chaplain Role
Military Environment

The individual that volunteers for service as a military chaplain will be required to follow the policies and procedures established by that military branch of service. Chaplain training will be required, and once the chaplain completes the training, absolute compliance with the policies and procedures become essential.

Chaplain Credentials
Essentially Important

When an individual enters into the chaplaincy ministry or takes on a position as a chaplain, the person's credentials should meet credibility standards without discrimination in any form. Also, the individual must be ecclesiastically and educationally qualified. There is no place in the chaplaincy for "diploma mill" credentials. *All* credentials must be verified through a system of checks and balances.

The functional role of a chaplain is an important one. Therefore, the chaplain must earn the respect of those being served. While earning that respect, the chaplain must become a trusted and functional member of the staff. The role covers a lot of territory, and to have the chaplain serve as the religious representative or advisor, a proven track record must be established. Once this track record has been developed, there will be a trust and respect established that will last a long time. To maintain the professional status of a productive chaplain, self-development must continue.

Therefore, as the chaplain continues to develop and to reach out to help people in this important role, he or she must become an active team player. And, as an active team player, the chaplain must be professionally prepared mentally, educationally and psychologically to perform the tasks encountered.

To be prepared professionally; what does this mean? And, why should a chaplain be prepared? Well, it's very simple to understand. Civic groups, law enforcement, hospitals/nursing facilities, veteran organizations and the military (active duty and volunteer) establish chaplain qualifications. How the process operates, and to what degree the selection reflects getting the best candidate for the position, is questionable. The selection criteria for a volunteer position is usually decided by the candidate's popularity or personal references submitted. The volunteer candidate selected usually is:

- a person of good character;
- a close friend of some members;
- a person usually active in church, or
- a minister with little or no education beyond high school.

However, when the same groups mentioned in the previous paragraph are interviewing or considering someone as a chaplain candidate for employment, the requirements for the position are more demanding. The chaplain candidate must meet strict eligibility requirements. An example of specific requirements are chaplain qualifications.

Chaplain Qualifications
Active duty Appointment
Volunteer for State Militia/Guard/Defense Force

Age: Age requirements (active duty). *Volunteer: Age requirements are flexible.*

Citizenship: U.S. citizen.

Physical: Physical standards. *Volunteer: Fit for service (exam by doctor).*

Minimum Education: BA/BS degree consisting of 120 semester hours credits from an accredited college or university. *Volunteer: Same educational requirements for clergy.*

Special Requirements: Must be a graduate of an accredited school of theology or a graduate of a university with a master of divinity degree or equivalent consisting of at least 90 semester hour credits. *Volunteer: Ministerial/*

pastoral experience is considered as a waiver option (considered on an individual basis).

Ecclesiastical Endorsement: Must be ordained and recommended by a recognized ecclesiastical endorsing agency registered with the Department of Defense. *Volunteer: Same ecclesiastical endorsement required.*

Moral Character: Be able to receive a favorable National Agency check. *Volunteer: All clergy must meet the same moral character background check.*

Pastoral/Ministerial Experience: A minimum of two years experience. *Volunteer: Same.*

Personal Character References: Three letters of character reference required. *Volunteer: Same.*

Appointment: The grade/rank commissioned or staff position assigned is determined by education, pastoral experience, and previous military service, et cetera. *Volunteer: Same.*

Note: All chaplain credentials must be verifiable. The professional status of the chaplain must be maintained, and the qualifiers met without exception. Administrators interested in hiring chaplains or staffing volunteer chaplains will require that all applicants complete an application, enclose a personal resume and have personal references.

These procedures are usually followed by law enforcement agencies, hospital/nursing facilities, correctional facilities and the military. If an individual is interested in getting involved in an official volunteer military organization (coming under a state's adjutant general command), and the educational requirements are not met, the volunteer *can* enroll in a college program, called distant learning, and earn the college credits needed. Also, he/she can receive a ministerial license and be ordained. For information, please contact the author for assistance.

Special Note: There is no way officials will water down the educational qualifiers and waive the selection criteria by allowing someone not qualified to become a chaplain. In the same vein, it is not possible to have a chaplain candidate become a chaplain without receiving the approval of the prospective chaplain's religious faith group. The qualifications and the reasons behind having strict requirements to become a chaplain must be completely understood by the applicant. There are *no* waivers granted on ecclesiastical endorsements, education, moral character or FBI record checks.

For those individuals interested in becoming a chaplain, but do not meet the chaplain requirements, they are encouraged to study to show themselves worthwhile. Once the qualifications are met, the interested chaplain prospect must reapply to be considered as a chaplain.

Personal Calling

There are chaplain applicants that have "God's calling" on their lives. They have the ecclesiastical endorsement by their recognized denomination. They have an outstanding character record, and their integrity is beyond reproach. All requirements are met except *education*! The door of opportunity *will not open*. Why? Simply, the educational requirement—education beyond high school—is not met.

A sincere desire and special interest in the chaplain ministry are positive attributes for a prospective chaplain. However, the door to the ministry will remain closed until all educational requirements are satisfactorily met.

The chaplain prospect must evaluate the basic requirements, reevaluate the "chaplain calling," and if the desire remains . . . qualifying becomes the first order of business.

Going back to school becomes necessary. There is no other alternative. The cost in time and money are factors one can not overlook. Is it worth the educational journey? Questions must be answered!

What most people probably do not know, and most often, really don't have an interest in, is the "personal calling" of an individual chaplain, or an individual who may have a desire to become a chaplain. Chaplains can be seen serving and performing duties and responsibilities in such places as:

- Churches
- Civic Organizations
- Correctional Facilities
- Hospitals
- Law Enforcement Agencies
- Military
- Nursing Homes
- Veteran Organizations

People functioning outside the chaplain vocation probably have no idea what the personal calling of an individual into the chaplaincy really is all about. The reasoning behind this "no idea" claim can be summed up by one most important statement: the calling does not come from man, it has to come from God. No person, other than the individual being called, has say-so in the matter. It's a spiritual calling. It's a special calling to do God's work. And, to become a chaplain, there must have been an earlier call from the Lord to become a Christian . . . something we refer to as the "salvation call."

When the individual first responded to the calling from God, and entered the ministry, the person probably found normal pastoral life very fulfilling and rewarding.

However, not all clergy get involved in an actual church or parish ministry. It does not take long to find oneself yearning for a "field white unto harvest." Usually the yearning will cause the person to look at a chaplaincy position in a prison or jail setting, a hospital, or so forth. But, for the young at heart, there is usually a serious look toward the military chaplaincy.

If age were not a factor, I would encourage the young educated person with a definite calling upon their life to take a serious look at entering the military chaplaincy. It is a career that will provide a worldwide ministry at the expense of the United States military department. You can broaden your education, and take the Word of God to locations around the world. But, most of all, while you serve the calling of God, you will be able to serve your country by ministering to nonmilitary and military people of all religious faiths. It has been stated that the military chaplaincy has the capability to have many religious faiths come into one setting and speak . . . *unbelievable* . . . Mormons, Greeks, Pentecostal Christians, Jews, Roman Catholics and Muslims participate. The barriers come down! This becomes a real sharing of faith. The chaplaincy is the place for opportunity to work for the Lord.

No debate is necessary to arrive at an understanding and agreement that to perform the work of a chaplain, one must be converted through a crisis encounter with God. The battle line is drawn at that point. The battle is fought and won at this crossroad in one's life. The war of repentance is fought and won at this juncture in one's life before moving on. But, once the spiritual salvation call has been responded to in a positive manner, it will be followed by an "obedience calling." This is a call to be faithful. A call to be loyal. And, most importantly, there is the call to prepare oneself. "Study to show thyself approved unto God, a workman that needeth not to be ashamed, rightly dividing the word of truth." (2 Tim. 2:15)

Someone of record has stated, "You do not need to prepare yourself, the Lord will tell you what to say." Yes, that is absolutely true. The Lord does speak to His servants; it is through His Word, called the Bible.

Personally, I have never heard the Lord speak audibly to me, in the same manner as we human beings speak to each other. But, I have had His Holy Spirit impress upon my spirit His direction for my life. Evidence to defend my case? I have none. However, if one could hear the actual voice of God say anything at all as they try to enter the ministry without preparation and studying, He probably would say something like this: "You are not prepared."

Men of great intellect and authority working in big business have determined that it is wise to have a chaplain on staff. The military decided a long time ago that chaplains are needed! Therefore, it becomes the chaplain's responsibility to perform their duties in an outstanding and professional manner. Thus, when this is done, nothing better will serve to establish the chaplain as a trusted and respected representative of God. An old saying has been handed down, "You have to win people to yourself before you can win them unto the Lord."

(L–R) Chaplains Maj. Ronald Street, Maj. Robert Forner, a personal friend WO3 Jack Williams, Grooms, LTC Gerald Harrison and Cpt. Randolph Gurley at the Brigadier General Promotion Ceremony.

Courtesy of Mrs. Betty Grooms

✝

Chapter Six:

THE MILITARY DEPARTMENT COMMAND STRUCTURE AND THEIR FUNCTION

Commanding General/Admiral

The military departments of different states (National Guard, Air National Guard, State Guard/State Militia/State Defense Force) are under the command of each state's adjutant general, and the military departments of the United States (Air Force, Army, Coast Guard, U.S. Marine Corps and Navy, including Military Reserve units of the same) are commanded by a Commanding General or Admiral. The Commanding General/Admiral is responsible for the religious life, morality, and morale of the command. The Commanding General/Admiral will have, under his/her command, a Chief of Chaplains. The Chief of Chaplains will have, under his/her command, subordinate chaplains.[18]

Chief of Chaplains and Subordinate Chaplains

As a member of the Commanding General/Admiral's staff, the Chief of Chaplains is the commander's staff advisor and consultant in the field of chaplaincy expertise. The Chief of Chaplains will provide the commander and staff with advice, information, programming and funding data, recommendations and plans concerning religion, morality, chaplain support activity, and chaplain personnel matters. The chaplain subordinates assigned to other commands in the organization will also function as members of the commander's staff, and provide to their commander the same categories of support as the Chief of Chaplains provides to the Commanding General/Admiral.

The Chief of Chaplains will have direct supervision of the chaplains at their command headquarters, but provides staff direction to subordinate chaplains at their assigned command level. It is important to note that the purpose of staff supervision is to assist the subordinate command and to enable the unit chaplain to provide accurate information to their commander and staff. The Chief of Chaplains must respect the subordinate chaplain's commander and work through the commander when requests are made to the chaplain. This will avoid conflict with any previous orders given to the subordinate chaplain by their commander. Establishing a command relationship will enhance the success of the religious program, and not place the subordinate chaplain in an embarrassing or compromising situation.

Standard Operating Procedures

The Chief of Chaplains will be responsible for establishing a Standard Operating Procedure (SOP). The SOP is a set of instructions, having the force of orders, which cover those features of operations that lend themselves to a definite or standardized procedure without loss of effectiveness. It states the desires of the Commanding General/ Admiral and covers policy, guidance, areas of special emphasis and expedient measures. An example of specific areas covered are:

- General Information
- Religious Services and Facilities
- Religious Education
- Pastoral Care
- Chaplain Support Activities
- Personnel
- Management and Funds
- Training
- Equipment and Supplies
- Reports
- Administration
- Organizational Chart and Job Descriptions
- Alert and Emergencies
- Briefings/Meetings

Consequently, when we understand what a chaplain is, with all of the delegated and designated specifics, and how the chaplain fits into the overall picture, the mission of the chaplaincy is made much clearer. It is from this platform that I find it necessary to identify and elaborate on the importance of having a structured "must be followed and respected" chain of command, a Standard Operating Procedure, and the chaplain mission.

It is commonly understood that any organization must have leaders *and* followers. The military chaplaincy, as an official part of the military, is no different. Leaders are selected, assigned an agenda, and delegated authority to perform assigned duties and responsibilities such as:
- the establishment of required administrative procedures,
- the formulation and organization of the chain of command,
- the creation of job descriptions listing the duties and responsibilities (chaplains and staff personnel),

- using an evaluation procedure to measure job performance for assignment and/or promotion (chaplain and staff),
- the establishment of a SOP, with a built-in methodology for periodic review/revision,
- formulating an annual training and continuing education plan, and
- a response callback to duty in times of an emergency, declared by command action.

The above listed duties and responsibilities are first put into effect and practice by the organization's Chief of Chaplains. The Chief of Chaplains is the highest ranking chaplain in a particular military organization, be it Army, Air Force, Coast Guard, and Navy (included in these same branches of service are personnel serving in the Reserves, Army National Guard, Air National Guard, et cetera). There are no chaplains serving in the U.S. Marine Corps; their chaplain is a Navy chaplain. Serving under the Chief of Chaplains are subordinate chaplains serving as the ranking Installation or Base Chaplains. Serving under the Installation Chaplain or Command Chaplain are subordinate chaplains serving in regiments, battalions, and brigades.

Therefore, the Chief of Chaplains will establish an SOP, inclusive of all religious support directives relating to administrative procedures, preparation of organizational and functional charts, the maintenance of an up-to-date chaplain SOP, and the guidelines/procedures of emergency plans. The Chief of Chaplains supervises and provides staff direction to the religious activities in subordinate commands. It is the responsibility of the chaplain to perform their chaplain's duties in accordance with the best principles of administration and personnel management. This involves coordination of all religious activities within the command, including supervision of chaplain staff. Secondly, the subordinate chaplain will be held responsible for incorporating the religious program procedures into their command's religious SOP as directed, following the SOP guidelines established and distributed by the Chief of Chaplains.

The chaplain serving on all command levels must be aware that the commander is the commanding officer, and it is required that the chaplain, as a member of the commander's staff, will serve as an advisor and consultant to the commander on religious affairs. The chaplain will provide the commander and staff with:

- advice and information,
- recommendations and plans concerning religion and morality,
- the Chaplain Religious Plan and Religious Program,
- personnel related business (religion, morals and morale).

It is a known fact that when the chaplain exhibits an interest in the command's mission, the chaplain will earn the confidence and support of the commander, the commander's staff, subordinate chaplains, and other military personnel. The success of the chaplain's religious plan and program is almost always dependent upon the support of the commander. Therefore, the chaplain must plan the religious program and then convince the commander of the merit of implementing it.

The pressure is on the chaplain to get along with the commander; therefore, the overall objective is to have successful accomplishments. The outcome of those accomplishments will be determined by how well the chaplain formulates the plans through staff procedures, and not through personal contact. A working relationship with the commander and his staff is to be established and maintained if success is to follow the chaplain.

The chaplain serves as a representative of God, and as long as the chaplain serves as God's spokesperson they must maintain a respect for another person's choice of religion, even if the chaplain has strong objections to that faith group's religious demeanor.

With the protection of the First Amendment of the United States Constitution—freedom of religion—the chaplain is guarded from being forced or diplomatically persuaded by any person or group of persons, regardless of authority line, to deviate from their religious faith group's beliefs and practices. The chaplain's message is to be purposely designed to bring spiritual values and guidance to military personnel and their families, retired military personnel and their families, and the civilians authorized to receive the chaplain's assistance. As a chaplain, an individual will have the awesome opportunity to serve God and country, and at the same time minister to people in diverse and dynamic settings.

The chaplain is a qualified professional person on a *mission*. That mission is spiritual care for people. To place priority on accomplishing the mission, the chaplain will discover that the terrain where the chaplain is needed is in such places as churches, civic organizations, correctional facilities, hospitals, law enforcement agencies, nursing homes, and veteran groups. Beyond the perimeter of civilians, the armed forces of the United States and its counterparts (National Guard, Military Reserve components and approved State Guards/State Defense Forces/State Militias) are prime targets for fulfilling the mission.

The chaplain's main ministry, militarily, is to:
- conduct religious services,
- provide pastoral counseling,
- give spiritual leadership through example,
- supply religious education,
- facilitate the worship of religious faiths other than their own,
- serve people of many religious backgrounds, and
- work in a truly interfaith surrounding.

It must be understood from the very beginning that the individual choosing to become a chaplain must meet specific ecclesiastical and educational requirements, and, most importantly have a spiritual calling from God. The chaplain prospect must have a sincere goal-oriented desire to begin this highly competitive process that leads toward fulfilling the Apostle Paul's recommendation to "study to show yourself approved unto God."

There must be an understanding of the mission of the chaplain, and once this meaning has been determined, the chaplain's "steps are ordered by the Lord."

✝

Chapter Seven:

CHAPLAIN OUTREACH MINISTRY RELATIONSHIPS

Establishing Relationships: Civilian and Military

The chaplaincy is a ministry for nonmilitary people and their families, as well as the military and their families. The chaplaincy is to provide the services of a chaplain on a twenty-four hours a day, seven days a week basis. Those services provided are reduced to two categories. One category is spiritual guidance and counseling. The second category is the offering of comfort in times of crisis. In addition, the chaplain is expected to celebrate the sacraments or minister the ordinances to help build a religious foundation which will contribute to the individual's spiritual maturity.

The chaplaincy is a dynamic environment where priests, ministers, and rabbis welcome the challenge of reaching out to nonmilitary and military personnel and their families of various backgrounds, cultures and religions. The overall objective is to bring spiritual depth to their lives. For those persons, having someone such as a chaplain to turn to when they are facing a crisis experience, or when they are having to cope with everyday stress and pressure on or off the job, can make a tremendous difference in their lives. It is the responsibility of the *chaplain* to be convinced, beyond a doubt, that the chaplain can and will make that difference. The *difference* is derived from the help furnished by and through almighty God.

The choice and decision one makes to become a chaplain is not like changing one's vocation because of some type of problem such as wages, labor requirements or management. It's not like changing garments, when you like one outfit better than the other. Having to deal with the call to His service is much more serious, and the service one is considering is a very unique mission assignment.

The professional clergyperson that chooses the spiritual care ministry (chaplaincy), and is motivated because of the possibility of reaching out to *all* men and women everywhere, nonmilitary and military, has a big job to accomplish. It becomes so important that the individual must count the costs before entering the chaplaincy. The preparation time and involvement will test the very fiber one is made of before the status of "seasoned chaplain veteran" has been reached.

There are many religious faiths one will encounter throughout the ministry. Therefore, a basic knowledge of other religious faiths, many of which are vastly different from one's own, is needed to be able to communicate with a mind of understanding.

Chaplains in a Pluralistic Society

Spoken prayer is common on many civic occasions such as civic meetings, legislative sessions, graduations, political rallies, testimonial dinners and community forums. Prayer in settings which are primarily secular should bind a group together in common concern. However, it can become divisive, even if not intended, when forms of language exclude some persons.

Individuals who lead the general community in prayer have a responsibility to be clear about the purpose as well as the nature of the occasion. Prayer on behalf of the general community should be general prayer. General prayer is inclusive, non-sectarian and carefully planned to avoid embarrassments and misunderstandings. Those who are reluctant to offer general prayer should be given the option of declining an invitation.

General public prayer on civic occasions is authentic prayer that also enables people to recognize the pluralism of American society. Prayer of any kind may be inappropriate on some civic occasions. Decisions should show respect both for public diversity and for the serious nature of prayer.

General prayer seeks the highest denominator without compromise of conscience. The prayer calls upon God on behalf of the particular public that has gathered, and it avoids individual petitions. Some prayers are opened by saying, "Mighty God," "Our Maker," or "Creator and Sustainer." At the closing of prayer one may use, "Hear our prayer Lord," "In Thy Name," "May goodness flourish," or simply, "Amen." Other alternatives can be used such as, "A moment of silent prayer."

When we are asked to pray and accept the invitation, we have a responsibility to understand that we have been asked to add a reminder of God's holy presence and to challenge people to touch Him by faith. We do not preach or make it a time to confess our faith.

The chaplains wear the cross or tablets, which identify the chaplain as Christian or Jew. In public we have the opportunity to say that our religion, Christianity and

Judaism, teaches us to care for others, regardless of their origin. Whatever a public prayer should be, it should not be cruel or uncaring. One of the most general prayers in the Bible is Psalm 117, the Bible's shortest book:

> O' Praise the Lord, all you Nations;
> Praise Him all you peoples;
> For His Love for you is great;
> And the truth of the Lord endures forever.
> Hallelujah.

The chaplain will minister in a pluralistic setting (a condition of society in which numerous distinct ethnic, religious, or cultural groups co-exist) by working with different religious faith groups of the Christian tradition and facilitating for the needs of others, such as ministering or preaching the Word, celebrating the Lord's Supper, conducting Bible studies, and providing counseling on quality-of-life issues.

Respect for Other Religious Faith Groups
Catholic

The chaplain may be of Roman Catholic faith. Catholics believe in the teachings of Jesus Christ and gather weekly to celebrate the Mass, a ritual of prayer and communion accentuated by song that is considered to be one of the most beautiful of all religious worship services.

At the heart of Catholic social issues are the protection of the life and dignity of the human person, caring for the poor and vulnerable, protecting and sustaining the environment, and a general commitment to the common good. In most of these churches, Mass is generally conducted several times on Sunday, along with a Mass offered on Saturday evenings. The priest provides a dynamic and diverse ministry, such as Eucharist celebration, baptism, penance and reconciliation, matrimony counseling, and pastoral care.

Protestant

The Protestant faith is composed of churches such as Assembly of God, Charismatic Episcopal Church, Church of the Brethren, Church of God, Episcopal Church, International Pentecostal Holiness Church, Lutheran Church, Presbyterian Church, Seventh-Day Adventist, Southern Baptist Church, Southern Methodist Church, United Pentecostal Church, United Methodist Church—the list goes on with nearly too many to name. All of these Protestant religious branches uphold the teachings of Jesus Christ; however, there are variations in leadership, worship, and biblical interpretation. They uphold the Bible as God's Word, believing that Jesus Christ died for the sins of the world, then arose from the dead. They also believe in the importance of the conversion of others to Christianity through missionary programs. A great deal of their energies are spent assisting the needy and performing community works. Most Protestant churches meet for services on Wednesdays, Sunday mornings and Sunday evenings and consist of traditional Bible studies followed by worship.

Greek Orthodox

Dynamic faith, limitless love and unbreakable unity characterize the ideals of the Greek Orthodoxy. As indicated by its name, the church's origins hail from the ancient Mediterranean area, which holds a distinct place in history as the former epicenter of civilization. They believe in the teachings of Jesus Christ and exercise three disciplines to assist them on their spiritual journey: watchfulness, to guard against social evils; prayer, as a means of communicating with God; and fasting, as a means of bringing the body together with the mind in contemplation of God's will. The church is dedicated to assisting the needy through the donation of food, money and manpower.

Judaism

Steadfast and faithful, followers of Judaism are proud of their heritage. Judaism is more of a civilization than just a religion. Jewishness is determined by parental heritage and personal identification. The main objectives of the Jewish community are to repair the broken pieces of the world so that the religious views of each person are afforded equal dignity and respect.

The Jewish community needs specific religious guidance that only a rabbi can offer, and the services they provide include High Holy Day services, a Brit Milah (circumcision for a baby boy, a naming ceremony for a girl), Bar and Bat Mitzvah Confirmation for thirteen- to fourteen-year-old boys or girls, confirmation for reformed children, weddings and Aufruff (a special ceremony for the groom), death, burial and Shivah mourning time (seven days) of a close relative, et cetera. Rabbis' responsibilities usually include serving a widespread area, in addition to their own ministry area; they travel to visit small Jewish communities, or train "lay leaders" to conduct services or teach classes on their own.

Mormon

Members of the Church of Jesus Christ of Latter-Day Saints are known as Mormons. Their mission is to share the message of Jesus Christ with every man, woman and child. In addition to biblical studies, Mormons use other texts to teach the principles of life, most notably, the *Book of Mormon*, which is another testament of Jesus Christ said to carry an account of Christ's visit to His "other sheep," the inhabitants of the North American Continent.

One of the most outstanding qualities of the Mormon people is their dedication to the family. Members are encouraged to work together toward spiritual goals within the structure of their families while striving to balance the many components present in daily living in order to spend as much time together as possible. The first priorities are to teach members to increase in faith and prayer, study the Scripture as a family activity, obey and keep the commandments, love and serve one another and reach out to others in need (to help the needy members they are encouraged to fast for twenty-four hours once a month, then donate to the needy all the money they would have normally spent on food for that day).

Islam

Islam was once considered an Eastern religion, but it is now beginning to take a more dominant role throughout the world with 1.4 billion followers. It was born in the Middle Ages. The Prophet, Muhammad, is considered by the Muslim community to be the last of the prophets sent from Allah (Arabic for "God"). The Koran (Qur'an), a text which they accept as a complete record of God's word, is also their reference for living.

One of the distinguished aspects of the Islamic faith is their respect for the religious beliefs of others. They are taught not to stand in judgment of their fellow men. It is *not* the practice of Muslim people to attempt to convert anyone to their faith. The individual interested in the Muslim faith must continue on his/her journey and come to the Muslim faith by his/her own personal decision to do so. The people of the Muslim faith place Moses and Jesus Christ in very high esteem. They usually meet every evening for prayer, and on Sunday night everyone gathers for an evening of dinner and discourse.

Baha'i

The Baha'i religion was founded by the nineteenth century prophetic figure, Baha'u'llah, and has six million followers. The teachings of Baha'u'llah promote the essential unity of all humanity, and assert that its well-being and security will be attained when that unity is established in each community throughout the world.

There are no clergy in the Baha'i faith, though spiritual gatherings are conducted regularly. Three issues at the core of the Baha'i movement are racial unity, gender equality and universal education.

It is only natural that the diversity of the population is reflected in the ever-growing array of religious centers and houses of worship. A thorough directory of churches, synagogues and centers in many communities could fill the pages of an entire book. Other religious faith groups are Buddhism and Hinduism, et cetera.

Regardless of the religious faith group, clergy must be willing to break down the barriers that separate them from communicating with other religious faith groups. The individual clergyperson must be willing to be cross-trained on how to minister to other religious faith groups when their clergy is needed and not present.

The chaplaincy is a unique ministry that is purposely directed toward bringing spiritual values and guidance to nonmilitary and military personnel. No matter what the race, creed, nationality or religious faith group that a person belongs to, the chaplain must prepare to minister to the individual in need. The religious services conducted by the chaplain provide pastoral counseling, give spiritual leadership, supply religious education, and facilitate the worship of faiths other than their own. The chaplain's vision should be to reach out to individuals for the purpose of enriching their lives morally and spiritually, and to encourage the establishment of a relationship with God. Energizing individuals with hope and strengthening them through pastoral care must be well planned by the ministry approach of the chaplain.

✝

Chapter Eight:

CHAPLAINS AND THE ETHICS CODE

Ethical and Unethical Behavior

Why are chaplains needed? Chaplains, who represent the chaplaincy, *must* conduct themselves in an ethical manner at all times. Chaplains make a difference. Chaplains are needed in civic organizations, law enforcement agencies, hospitals and nursing home facilities, jails/correctional institutions, veteran organizations, and official militias that come under the command of each individual state's adjutant general. The presence of chaplain/clergy have an untold affect upon an individual's behavior and encourages a respect for God. Also, individuals need counseling and assistance during times of difficult and stressful situations, especially when death is to be coped with. In addition, there are times when the clergy/chaplain is needed to give invocations, benedictions, perform wedding vows, participate in city, county, state and federal ceremonies, dedications and memorials to honor the deceased. The credibility of the chaplain goes a long way!

Ethics Code

Civilian Clergy/Chaplains

The chaplain who has accepted the call of God upon their life enters into a covenant with God to serve Him faithfully and honorably. The commitment to love God with the heart, soul, mind and strength, and to love thy neighbor as thyself is a covenant to obey His commandments as a loyal and faithful servant.

The challenge! Chaplains must enter into the ethics code of their own free will, with the understanding that they will not betray the trust and confidence of their ecclesiastical endorser, and will hold in trust the traditions and practices of their religious faith group. Chaplains must take a personal interest in and covenant the following:

- It is understood by me that I will be functioning as a chaplain in a pluralistic environment alongside fellow chaplains of other religious faiths. I further agree and understand that I am to provide chaplain ministry to all military personnel and their families entrusted to my care.
- I will respect the religious beliefs and traditions of other chaplains and the military personnel I am entrusted to minister to and work with. Furthermore, I will never disrespect the religious practices of those religious faith groups that are different than my own, but I will draw upon the beliefs, principles and practices that we have in common.
- I will, if in a supervisory position, respect the practices and beliefs of other chaplains, and I will exercise care not to require of them any service or practice that would be in violation of the faith practice of their particular faith group.
- I will seek to establish meaningful relationships with my family, fellow chaplains, staff personnel and military personnel.
- I will defend them against unfair discrimination on the basis of gender, race, religion, or national origin.

- Furthermore, I will not proselytize to any other religious faith group, but I retain the right to evangelize to those who are non-affiliated.
- I will maintain the confidentiality of privileged communication received during the performance of my ministry, and I will not disclose it in private or public.
- I will show personal love for God in my life and ministry as I strive together with other chaplains to preserve the dignity, maintain the discipline and promote the integrity of the profession to which I have been called.
- I will strive to maintain a disciplined ministry by keeping prayer and devotion a priority of my life, and endeavor to maintain good health habits by engaging in educational and recreational activities for professional growth and personal development.
- In conclusion, I recognize the special power afforded me by my ministerial office as a chaplain. I will never use that power in ways that violate the rights of another person, religiously, emotionally, or sexually. I will use the office of chaplain only for that which is best for the persons under my ministry, so help me God.

When are Chaplains Needed?

This question has been asked many times. There have been many answers. Some of the most important answers expressed in a recent personal survey related to both peacetime and wartime:

Military personnel should have access to a chaplain when personal problems are being experienced (family, supervisor relationships, alcohol/drugs, transfers, promotions, finances, et cetera).

However, the most important responses were related to war, death, being wounded, support for family and being away from family.

Military personnel and their families during peacetime, as well as in wartime, must have a quick response from the chaplain when problems come up or exist. But, when the military has been deployed or relocated to a war environment situation for an indefinite period of time, the chaplain becomes a valuable asset to all staff.

Throughout the history of America and our continued fight to preserve our freedom, liberty and religious rights, many lives have been sacrificed. The duties and responsibilities of chaplains have carried them into harm's way also. Their lives have been sacrificed, too. The community clergy deals with some of the same types of problems with their church congregations. They have to deal with deacon boards and many committees to carry on their ministry. But, I dare to say, not in the same fashion as a chaplain has to respond during his/her military career, especially during wartime. The chaplain is needed during peacetime, but it becomes a bit more serious when a war is going on. Let's review the military statistical record of our nation.

✟

Chapter Nine:

THE HISTORY OF WARS FOUGHT BY THE UNITED STATES

War Statistics

When death comes, the blood of the fighting men or women always comes out red . . . death has no respect for color, creed or nationality. Nor does it have respect for branch of service, position or rank. Included in the death statistics we find chaplains are casualties, too. The chaplain is no ordinary, prepared fighting person. No weapon is issued . . . only the tools of the trade are the issue . . . humanity wrapped in courage and honor. Throughout military records, the reports are spotted with acts of bravery by chaplains as defensive and offensive warfare were being waged. Chaplains have died on the battlefield performing their chosen profession. Also, chaplains have been wounded seriously performing their ministry of caring for the military family. As you examine the statistics, keep in mind how costly freedom is!

Throughout military history it has been recognized that religious services are a must for military personnel. George Washington realized that need in 1775. Washington's concern resulted in the Continental Congress approving the establishment of the Army chaplaincy on July 29, 1775. Also, the Navy adopted a policy that would ensure that "commanders of ships of the Thirteen United Colonies" would provide divine services for its personnel (U.S. Navy Regulations, adopted November 28, 1775). The Army and the Navy began their great history by incorporating within their command a religious ministry that made it possible for military personnel to practice their religion. It was a guarantee that individuals serving in the military would not be deprived of opportunities for the free exercise of their religious faith.

It has always been understood by the men and women serving in the military of the United States of America, no matter what branch one serves in, that there is the possibility of life-threatening situations. Since the beginning of American history, many have fought to preserve freedom. That fighting has resulted in many being wounded, and many have died on the battlefield, at sea, and in the air. The fighting originally took place on American soil, but to preserve that liberty, fighting has taken America's best to countries around the world to help others acquire liberty and freedom.

After 28 years of associated military service, having served in many job classifications, military history facts have been interesting to me. The statistical data found below are credited to the American War Deaths website.[18]

Principle U.S. Wars
- Between 1775 and 1991, American military forces have been involved in war action or conflicts 54 times on American soil and in countries around the world.

- Over 38,290,000 participants have been involved.

- There have been 1,081,000 deaths.

- There are approximately 16,146,000 veterans still living (estimated statistics as of 1999); of this number,
  - ❖ 35 percent participated in WWII,
  - ❖ 18 percent were involved in the Korean Conflict,
  - ❖ 40 percent fought in Vietnam, and
  - ❖ 7 percent participated in other conflicts/wars.

- At least 500,000 veterans die each year.

As we review these military statistics, especially the number of personnel reported to have served in the military, one of the most important decisions made in 1775 by the Continental Congress was prompted by General George Washington. He was instrumental in getting approval to make chaplains a part of the Army. Establishment of the chaplaincy was passed and approved on July 29, 1775 by the United States government. The chaplains of 1775 performed their duties in the military in an above-average manner, and they continue to do so in today's military. Chaplains are needed!

There have always been sacrifices of life, property and reputation made by a people who desired to have freedom. It began when the first individual set foot on North American soil in 1620. Defending themselves and the community they lived in was just a way of life for our early forefathers. More and more people came to North America as early settlers. Up and down the east coast, borders were established as colonies, later to become states. By the middle 1600s the colonies organized themselves into a defense force, manned to protect and defend their pursuit for freedom and liberty.

Home guards or home militias were established, armed, uniformed and trained. Young men, as young as fifteen or sixteen years old, and old men, as old as sixty to sixty-five, all volunteered to help keep their communities safe and secure. All was not lost by leaving England, the militias patterned themselves militarily after the British model. If the fight was not against the Indians, it was against the British, French or Spanish. Freedom carried with it a high price, and in the middle of all of the military activities were the community clergy . . . the clergy preached on the Sabbath and fought on the day after. The citizen-soldier-preacher could be relied upon to be involved.

Revolutionary War
Dead	4,435
Wounded	8,445
Cost	$101,000,000
Participants	290,000

The American Revolution (1775-1783) was a conflict between the British colonies in North America and their parent country, Great Britain. The war was a war of independence and a war to establish a republican form of government, in which the people would have representative say so. To gain independence cost many lives during the war, and given a part in that war were community clergy, chaplains. Many of the military were not members of a church. Of those who had religious affiliation, the majority were of the Protestant faith.

When the call went out for volunteer clergy to join General George Washington's Continental Army, Reverend William Emerson of Concord, Massachusetts was the first to arrive. On July 29, 1775 the Continental Congress established the chaplaincy, and Chaplain William Emerson was honored as the first chaplain of the Revolutionary War (Emerson died while still on active duty as a chaplain). However, there were representatives of many religious faiths present, including Catholics, Quakers, Dutch Reformers, Mennonites, and Anglicans. The field of labor was wide open for the chaplain to perform the chaplain duties and to learn firsthand of other religious faiths. In 1778, Benjamin Balch became the first American Navy Chaplain. Yes, chaplains were needed during this period of history, and they are needed now!

After the Revolutionary War was over in 1789, the governmental authorities decided there was no need to continue to have a large number of men serving in the Army. Therefore, military manpower was reduced to less than six hundred. There were no chaplains retained. Three years later, legislation authorized the appointment of one chaplain position. An Episcopalian clergy discharged after the war was appointed as the Army's only brigade chaplain (Chaplain John Hurt).

Between 1775 and 1783, 240 chaplains served the American cause. They served alongside the fighting men in campaigns at Bunker Hill, Quebec, White Plains, Princeton, Brandywine, Saratoga, Monmouth, Camden, and Yorktown. They performed their chaplain duties by accompanying soldiers to and from the battlefields, conducting religious services in the camps, visiting and caring for the sick and wounded, and ministering to the dying. Many made the supreme sacrifice. On January 2, 1777 Chaplain John Rosbrugh was the first chaplain to be killed in battle during the war (second Battle of Trenton).

The duties of chaplains varied, but as far as spiritual duties, they had the same responsibilities as at home. Although the chaplains received both praise and condemnation for their sermons, they all tried to see that the troops in their command, officers and enlisted, received proper spiritual guidance. It was just a normal thing for chaplains to do . . . the Catholic chaplains would hold religious services for Protestant soldiers, and Protestant chaplains would conduct religious services for Catholic troops.

Several years of joint cooperation while at war did more to decrease bigotry than fifty years in civilian life. The reason was that the men served together, fought together, and in some cases, died together. The barriers that separate people must be broken down, particularly for people who claim they love and follow God's Word, but cannot worship with another faith group. Loving God and loving your neighbor cannot be improved upon . . . the Lord stated this and we must obey the Word! Say "O' me" or say "Amen." It's the truth nevertheless! All chaplains must share this view regardless of denomination or sectarian lines.

War of 1812

Dead	2,260
Wounded	4,505
Cost	$90,000,000
Participants	287,000

Chaplain personnel files, stored at the War Department, of chaplains who had previously served in the military, were destroyed by a fire at the War Department in 1800. Also, other chaplain-type records were evidently destroyed by the British when the capital was burned in 1814. There were eleven chaplains that served in the War of 1812, and only one is known to have died in the war.

Mexican-American War

Dead	13,263
Wounded	32
Cost	$71,400,000
Participants	79,000

During the Mexican-American War (1846-1848) there were only eight civilian chaplains serving in all the Army, and none of them were able, by Army standards, to follow troops into the field. This led to serious neglect of the religious needs of military personnel, and the denial of their rights to free exercise of religion.

Note: In 1856, the adjutant general could not find any records related to chaplain military service prior to April 2, 1813. However, as many as 175-275 chaplains continued to serve in state militias.

Civil War

Dead	563,120
Wounded	418,200
Cost	$5,183,000,000

The Civil War of 1861-1865 saw the number of chaplains increase, and for the first time there were chaplains of other religious faiths ministering alongside Protestant chaplains, such as Jews, Native Americans, and the first black chaplain. Chaplains have always distinguished themselves in battle-raging situations. For example, a Catholic chaplain (William Corby) administered the last rites to the dying under a fierce exchange of weapon firing, giving a General Absolution to over five hundred men just a short time before they were killed on the battlefield at Gettysburg. The Chaplain Corby statue is erected on the field at Gettysburg on Cemetery Ridge.

Three Army chaplains won the Distinguished Medal of Honor for heroics during the Civil War. They were John Whitfield, from Indiana (1862); Francis Hall, from Tennessee (1863); and Milton Haney, from Indiana (1864).

Veteran's grave in the National Cemetery,
San Francisco, California.

Burials: 1800-Present
Veterans buried at the National Cemetery,
San Francisco, California.

Veterans buried at the National Cemetery,
San Francisco, California.

North

Dead	363,020
Wounded	281,100
Participants	2,213,000

Research estimates reveal that 2500-3000 chaplains served the Union Army. One chaplain, Colonel Milton Haney, was awarded the Congressional Medal of Honor for bravery during the taking of Atlanta, Georgia.

Army chaplains also distinguished themselves during the Civil War as combatants. (In 1882, chaplains were to be non-combatants as constrained by the Geneva Convention.) Some 90-100 chaplains of the North served in a combat role prior to their appointment as chaplains, and some went from chaplain to regular Army status as line officers. It was reported that former chaplain William Pile of Missouri, an infantry officer (1861), distinguished himself in the war and was discharged as a major general.

South

Dead	199,110
Wounded	137,100
Participants	1,000,000

Research estimates reveal that 650-1100 chaplains served in the Confederate Army.

Spanish-American War

Dead	2,893
Wounded	1,637
Cost	$283,200,000
Participants	392,000

World War I
Dead	116,708
Wounded	204,002
Cost	$18,676,000,000
Participants	4,744,000

It is estimated that 3,350 U.S. service personnel are still listed as missing in action (MIA) from WWI.

When the United States entered WWI on April 6, 1917, there were 74 regular Army and 72 activated National Guard chaplains. By the end of the war on November 11, 1918, there were a total of 2,363 chaplains.

The chaplains began to make great strides as a needed chaplaincy branch of the military under the faithful support of another supportive general, General John J. "Blackjack" Pershing.

During WWI, chaplains were among the highest number of casualties. Their heroism is reflected in the estimated war statistics, which were:

- 5 killed in action
- 6 died of wounds
- 12 died from disease or accident
- 27 others wounded in action
- 5 awarded the Distinguished Service Medal
- 23 awarded the Distinguished Service Cross
- 15 awarded the Silver Star
- 57 received decorations from allied foreign nations, including 16 Croix de Guerre, and 1 Belgian War Cross.

Also, during WWI, the Congressional Medal of Honor was awarded to 72 military persons for bravery.

In 1920, the Office of Chief of Chaplains was enacted by public law, known as the Capper Act.

Between 1923 and 1930 the chaplaincy came under the attack of high brass again, resulting in the number of chaplains being reduced to 125 Regular Army chaplains and a few reserve chaplains.

The 1923 Conference on Morals and Religious Work in the Army began a long look at the duties and responsibilities of chaplains. Reports from the conference stated:

> The purposes of our government in appointing chaplains and the place of religion in the Army have been misunderstood. The misunderstanding came about because frequently a chaplain has been used simply to promote what is known as morale. The chaplain does promote true morale in the best possibly way—"by religious sanction." When he is asked to promote morale first and religion afterwards, he is asked to be false to his mission.

World War II

Dead	407,316
Wounded	670,846
Cost	$262,259,000,000
Participants	16,535,000

It is estimated that 78,750 U.S. service personnel are still listed as missing in action from WWII.

WWII proved to be the breakthrough for the chaplaincy in terms of numerical growth, acceptance from military leadership, clarification of chaplains' ministry roles, and acquiring desperately needed chapel facilities.

In 1940 there were 382 Army chaplains on active duty, and 93 chaplains in the Navy. By the end of WWII a total of 9,117 chaplains served in the Army and 2,934 chaplain served in the Navy. They represented 71 religious denominations.

The Lord sent other generals to help the chaplaincy do its job religiously. Chaplain William Arnold, Army Chief of Chaplains, led the way by soliciting help from General Hap Arnold, a close friend of General Dwight Eisenhower, and General George C. Marshall, to protect his chaplains from the distractions of secular duties (like being assigned as library officers, athletic officers, et cetera). President Roosevelt was also concerned for the spiritual welfare of the military. He stated in 1942, ". . . we will never fail to provide for the spiritual needs of our officers and men under the chaplains of our armed forces."

Priority was given to conducting religious services. It was understood that no matter how busy a chaplain might be otherwise, the number one responsibility was to provide services so the personnel could worship God according to their particular faiths.

This action prompted the chaplain to follow a newly revised religious plan and program. The chaplaincy was divided into four main areas of ministry, and was to provide spiritual guidance acceptable to all faiths, conduct religious services, counsel with individuals, and visit throughout the command assigned. The four main areas were religious, military, pastoral, and community relations.

In March, 1942 the Army Air Force (AAF) was given 268 chaplains to serve their air group, and by July, 1942 the AAF decided on a name for their chaplains—Air Chaplain. By the end of WWII, 2,200 chaplains served in the AAF. The U.S.A.F. was unofficially being organized . . . and, on September 18, 1947, the U.S.A.F. was officially born.

On July 27, 1949, Chaplain Charles Carpenter was promoted to Major General and made the chief of U.S.A.F. chaplains. This ushered in a seven-fold religious program:

1. Worship . . . . ⎫
2. Pastoral ministry . . . . ⎬ 77% of time
3. Moral and religious education . ⎭
4. Counseling . . . . ⎫
5. Humanitarian services . . . . ⎬ 15 % of time
6. Cultural leadership . . . . ⎫
7. Public relations . . . . ⎬ 8 % of time

In December, 1948 another progressive step was made to provide protection for the chaplain when communication and counseling were conducted with military personnel. Due in large measure to religious traditions such as Roman Catholicism, in which communication between priest and penitent is protected by the priest to his death, the United States military extended this privilege to those counseling with chaplains of all faiths. All branches of the armed forces have the following required protection:

> The communication with a chaplain by any person made in the relationship of penitent and clergyman, either as a formal act of religion, as in the confessional, or one made as a matter of conscience to a chaplain in his

capacity as a clergyman, is a privileged communication. The chaplain cannot be obliged to disclose such communication.

Other noted accomplishments by WWII military personnel include the following:

- First black American pilot to shoot down an enemy plane: Captain Charles Hall, U.S. Air Corps.
- First black American pilot to shoot down a German jet plane: Captain Roscoe Brown, U.S. Air Corps.

Korean Conflict

Dead	33,651
Wounded	102,284
Cost	$67,386,000,000
Participants	6,807,000

It is estimated that 8,172 U.S. service personnel are still listed as missing in action (MIA) from the Korean War.

Chaplain Emil J. Kapaun, a Roman Catholic priest (8th Regiment of the 1st Calvary Division) was captured by the Chinese on November 2, 1950. While in captivity he ministered to many American soldiers under some of the most terrible conditions. Eventually, suffering from a blood clot, pneumonia and dysentery, he died as a prisoner on May 23, 1951. He was posthumously awarded the Legion of Merit for his courageous actions. Many chaplains were captured during the Korean War and none of them survived their internment.

Vietnam Conflict

Dead	58,168
Wounded	153,356
Cost	$150,000,000,000
Participants	9,200,000

It is estimated that 2,202 U.S. service personnel are still listed as missing in action from Southeast Asia.

Additional data:
- Chaplain Charles Watters (killed November 1967): awarded the Medal of Honor for bravery
- Chaplain Angelo Liteky (killed December 1967): awarded the Medal of Honor for bravery
- First African-American officer to lead Marines into battle in Vietnam: Major General J. Gary Cooper, U.S.M.C.

Vietnam Chaplain Statistics and Awards:
> 13 killed in action
> 2 awarded the Congressional Medal of Honor
> 719 awarded the Bronze Star
> 586 awarded the Army Commendation Medal
> 318 awarded the Air Medal
> 82 awarded the Purple Heart
> 66 awarded the Legion of Merit
> 26 awarded the Silver Star

Lebanon   268 Deaths

Grenada   19 Deaths

Panama   40 Deaths

Gulf War
Dead	363
Wounded	357
Cost	$61,100,000,000
Participants	400,000

Military battle deaths of personnel serving in the Army, Navy, Marines and Air Force from WWI, WWII, the Korean Conflict and Vietnam were:

Army: 18,462,000 participated	293,505
Navy: 7,202,466 participated	39,487
Marine Corps: 1,887,100 participated	39,545
Air Force: 3,025,000 participated	2,939

Other military items of interest:
- First African-American chaplain to attain the rank of General: Brig. Gen. Matthew A Zimmerman, a South Carolinian.
- First African-American American female to attain the rank of General in the U.S.A.F.: Brig. Gen. Marcelite Jordan-Harris
- First African-American American female astronaut: Dr. Mae C. Jemison

The Price of Freedom

Americans have gained their freedom and had their liberties guarded throughout the nation's history by courageous American men and women standing together, both at home and on foreign soil. But, Americans have had to pay a high price to win these liberties and remain free. The cost has been paid in blood . . . in death on the battlefield . . . in suffering at the scene of action . . . in hospitals . . . and at home during rehabilitation.

Now, there are two big decisions the U.S. Government must make regarding the veterans. Without reservations, the following are a must:

- The government must provide medical benefits and adequate retirement benefits for veterans.
- The government must provide a military funeral for the veteran when it is requested.

Chaplain History and Heritage Measured

The history and heritage of the military chaplaincy are measured by performance and reflect an interesting chronicle of service. The chaplains have made an indelible imprint and a deep, lasting impression on the lives of the men and women they ministered to in peace and war.

The United States of America and its military forces have been blessed beyond words of praise. This has always been the case in times of chaos, adversity and dismay on the home front, as well as difficulty on foreign soil.

The chaplain has moved out with the troops to fulfill the chaplain role and provide ministry to those in need. During times of conflict military leaders have always looked to the chaplain for religious support and spiritual guidance. It is during these times that the men and women serving in the military welcome the chaplain, and give way to their ministry. This is no exception!

The Bible records many events that have occurred in society and verifies the fact that priests and other religious persons were counted upon in times of war. An example of this is recorded in the Scriptures, in Deuteronomy 20:2-4 (The priests accompanied the troops to the battle scene). Then, there is another biblical example recorded in Joshua

6:5-6 (General Joshua had the priests involved in the success of taking Jericho). These Scriptures establish very good examples of a participatory-type of priestly service and ministry before the troops, and make an unbelievable public expression of loyal support of the leader.

Chaplains serving the military perform the chaplaincy ministry to personnel stationed in places all over the world—where language, cultural, and religious differences do not allow personnel access to participate in the practices of their individual religious faith.

The chaplain bridges the gap in providing chaplain access to the military personnel because:
- it guarantees free exercise of their religious faith,
- their duties keep them in dangerous areas or in harm's way,
- military personnel must not be denied the choice to practice their religious faith, or be denied access to a chaplain because of their assignment, and
- the greatest ministry performed by chaplains is discovered by just being nearby, in the view of others.

Chaplains present such a diversified background of personal ministry that it will never alter the fact that the chaplain will minister to others outside of their religious faith group.

When the chaplain's insignia is seen, others will only see through the eyes of their conception of a minister or clergyperson and never see the uniqueness of the chaplain's clerical position. Having and being aware that the chaplain is nearby communicates something, and means something to the sensitive person.

Chaplains have reported many short responses from the troops in passing that really express a sincere respect for the chaplain, such as, "Chaplain, it sure is good to have you pay us a visit." The chaplain may not have been in the area for the purpose of saying a prayer, giving a speech, or having to participate in a specific command function, but being in the area is important. The chaplain should never, for one moment, think that the presence of the chaplain and the visibility of the chaplain's insignia do not carry with them special meaning . . . they do!

The life of the chaplain contains no routine days. The day is filled with problems, and the order of the day is to provide necessary religious counseling for all military personnel and their families. Just like the community pastor has to deal with church business and church officials, the chaplain is required to take on the stressful stipulations and required directives of the chain of command.

When nearby, the chaplain can predict that military families will face fear, distress, skepticism, transition, and the constant awareness of death's reality in the same manner as community individuals and families. The chaplain and the community pastor/clergy are not superman-type individuals. They, too, have to fight physical, emotional, mental and spiritual warfare to stay stable and functional themselves. They fight the "fight of faith" to maintain their strength to be physically fit and spiritually strong in the battle for others! It is proper and accurate when someone may say, "For the chaplain to function under pressure, the calling of God upon the chaplain's life is a call to duty."

Memorial Day 1997

✝

Chapter Ten:

CHAPLAIN SURVIVAL TEST

Chaplains: Fighting the Bullets from Inside the System
Discrimination is the Ugly Word

The chaplain is not exempted from having to face unethical and unprofessional behavior by his/her superiors, subordinates, and other military personnel. Once the chaplain becomes aware of the negative behavior of any military person within the command, the decision must be made to advise the commander. The web of unwarranted and undeserving difficulty will weave itself around the chaplain so tightly that it will stress the chaplain beyond the ability to perform adequately. The chaplain cannot be a middle-of-the-road person. The chaplain must actively choose to be on the side of right versus simply standing against the wrong. When that action is taken, the chaplain puts himself in a no-win situation. At times, because of his stand, the chaplain will be conveniently overlooked for promotion or transferred for the best of the service. The act of standing up for what is right does carry with it a price, and most of the time the chaplain suffers! So sad! But true!

Many chaplains, because of their religious faith group "evangelical" ecclesiastical endorsements, have been evaluated by their non-evangelical religious faith groups superiors differently than they do chaplains of their particular faith groups. This action has resulted in premeditated discrimination against chaplains that hold their credentials with a "evangelical" faith group—denial of promotion, denial of assignments to supervisory chaplain positions, and even in many cases, early retirement! This is not restricted to just one branch of military service, it is practiced in all branches that have chaplains on staff.

In a real sense, if the "known" truth was accepted, the facts would bear out that some chaplain superiors associated with non-evangelical and some liturgical Protestant religions appear, by their actions, to have tried to create a "state church" by discriminating against chaplains of other religious faith groups that stress their "full gospel" beliefs openly and unashamedly. My personal identifiers, labeled as "CEL," are the most active group to appear to promote their agenda in an assertive manner against other chaplains. If you are a chaplain, or you have served as a chaplain, you come up with your own personal label and compare it with mine. It would be interesting to see if your label and mine have anything in common.

Protestant chaplains are more conservative and more evangelical, and it seems that because of identifiable factors that they are overlooked when it comes to promotion and consideration for leadership positions. And this must be stopped! Our military personnel are deprived of their religious rights because of this discrimination! Military personnel need and want religious guidance from their own religious faith group's chaplains when they have to deal with the difficulties experienced when deployed in harm's way. Chaplains are trained to give spiritual guidance to military personnel when they face life's problems and death. These spiritual implications become important as one thinks about dying. Religion has the answer. This was wisely considered by our forefathers who served in the first Congress when they drafted the Bill of Rights.

Examples of What Chaplains Have to Deal With:

1. Chaplain Referring to Jesus as a Bastard

2. Superior Suggestion: Do Not Put Things in Print

3. Discrimination Against a Religious Faith Group

4. Disrespect

Ministers, religious leaders and/or chaplains, no matter what denomination is represented, must realize that they do *not* have a monopoly on the manner in which the message of God is proclaimed. Nor do they have God's blessings for their unscrupulous tactics of discrimination against another religious faith or derogatory remarks made against the Name of Christ. God's method of getting his word promulgated is a method of inclusion, not exclusion.

In addition, I will cite three examples that were actually experienced by more than one chaplain, including myself. These examples are noted for the purpose of trying to prepare a chaplain for the warfare within the ranks, more so than from without. There will come a time when you will have to take a stand, and when you do, you can count your support on one hand. But, the principles of right against wrong, and righteousness against sinfulness, must be defended, even if it costs a promotion or leads to a change in assignment. The ministry and chaplains' fight is not against flesh and blood, it is against the darkness of evil. And, you can say what you will, but the clergy or chaplains that stand up for evil practices, or actually take part themselves, are at that point . . . in darkness. No two ways about it! Chaplains, at times, do practice evil against others. So sad, but nevertheless, it's true.

It has been the practice of some commanders, or chaplains who have been elevated to a command position or to a chaplain senior rank, to insulate themselves with well-planned, invisible prejudicial barriers to block out other religious faiths or identified chaplains of integrity from rising to leadership positions or rank within the military chaplaincy.

It is a known fact, as stated previously, that the military chaplaincy has been, for some time, under the controlled leadership of certain chaplains from particular denominations. You can check the history yourself and come up with your own list, but my personal observation, research and interviews with other chaplains reveal what I would call the "Dominating Three." You take a guess and solve the puzzle! The naming of the denomination is withheld to protect the innocent! The denomination is not the wrong party, it is the individuals of the denomination who perform in a questionable manner.

Sample Cases in Review
1. Christ Referred to As a Bastard

Once upon a time there was a southern state militia, consisting of over five hundred volunteer personnel, performing military duties and responsibilities. Included in this militia was a Chaplain Detachment consisting of twenty-five chaplains representing nine denominations associated with Catholic and Protestant religious faiths. The chaplains were young men, middle-age men, old men, and one female; twenty-four were white and one was non-white.

The command was led by an outstanding, military-experienced major general. His staff were also experienced men of integrity. The chaplains were individuals with character and dedication to promoting the cause of God and His Son, Jesus Christ—except one. This particular chaplain had some type of problem hidden beneath his projected faith in God. It seemed he would always try to debate any chaplain on the life of Christ. His attitude could be easily detected as anti-Christ.

Many of the chaplains, after they got to know him, would just keep their distance from him to avoid a debate. I don't know if that particular chaplain had experienced some personal discrimination during his regular military duty as an active duty chaplain or not. But, using only common reasoning, one would think that a chaplain who had received a commission in the military, had an ecclesiastical endorsement and was representing a Protestant religious denomination, surely would have no justifiable reason to label Christ as a bastard. He did though, and repeatedly. This was brought to the attention of the Senior Chaplain, but nothing seemed to stop the chaplain's continued stupid attitude. "Wait, it will go away," was the senior chaplain's remark when it was brought to his attention.

Many other chaplains tried to establish a relationship with the chaplain in question, but he did not seem to want any white friends. The Senior Chaplain had to take a leave of absence for personal reasons, and he appointed two of his senior chaplains to share supervisory responsibilities together. The annual training came up and all of the chaplains attended, except for this one disrespectful, problem chaplain. During the chaplain training, a class on problem solving was conducted. Every chaplain seemed to have gotten involved in the class discussion, and the number one problem that surfaced concerned the behavior of the absentee chaplain. The question: What could be done about the chaplain's disgraceful behavior?

It was suggested that a statement be drawn up outlining the chaplain's behavior as witnessed by those that would sign it. Every chaplain that personally heard the disgraceful remarks made by the problem chaplain against Christ signed the statement of agreement. The next step was to have the two chaplains acting as supervisory chaplains request an audience with the Commanding General via the chain of command. This was done. The case was brought to the attention of the commander, and he heard the case.

The commander reviewed the chaplains' statement of agreement and a discussion followed on the subject. The commander was a Christian himself and could not believe what had been going on, especially that he had not been informed earlier of the existing problem. The commander stated he would investigate this problem and take appropriate and immediate action.

The commander handled the incident via a counselling situation which resulted in transferring the chaplain to another position. However, the chaplain, without objection, moved to the non-chaplain position but continued to wear the cross. Later on follow-up action had to be taken by the commander, resulting in the chaplain finally removing the crosses from his uniform. Nothing was put into writing except what had been reported by the chaplains. Many of the chaplains tried to work with the former chaplain in his new position, but he would always be negative, and continued to openly express his negative feelings about Christ . . . his choice! So sad!

The point is, chaplains have to stand together when a problem affects the cause of God and His servants.

2. *Superior Suggestion: Do Not Put Things in Writing*

The problem discussed and used as example one provides the materials for example two.

The chaplains stood together to solve the problem with another chaplain, and the manner in which they went about it did not receive the support of a certain senior officer. Later, the senior officer called one of the involved supervisory chaplains into his office and gave him a lecture on when to and when not to put incidents into written form. He stated, "You should be careful and do not do that! It will cause more problems." Problems for whom? The chaplain explained why the decision was made and that other chaplains expressed their negative feelings about what had been done by the accused chaplain. The senior officer did not seem to buy that reasoning, and used no uncertain terms to express his dissatisfaction at the manner in which this problem was handled.

The chaplain left that counseling session with the feeling that the positive results would have been different if that senior officer had been the Commanding General! All of the chaplains became aware of that counseling session and were glad the problem was carried to the Commanding General and not to that particular officer. If that had been done, there would have probably been a cover-up of the facts to save the union!

Later on, that particular senior officer became a retirement statistic, as did the problem chaplain.

There are times when a chaplain will have to take a stand against unethical practices by a chaplain or a commander, no matter what the rank or position that chaplain or commander may hold. It is also true in the community church as well. Clergy will have to stand up against deacons, official church board member, when unethical practices or behaviors affect the church . . . standing alone many times. Many times you will be labeled as a "bad person" for taking a stand. It is not a comfortable position to find yourself in, nor is it popular. You may discover that those who at one time agreed to stand with you now for some reason find it convenient to follow at a distance. Those individuals lack courage, and may have chosen to stand back because of an upcoming promotional opportunity or perhaps just decided not to become involved! Nevertheless, you find yourself left alone to fight . . . surrounded by a swarm of killer bees, in a den of snakes, or hung out to dry! You then, "fight the bullets."

Please don't get me wrong; other chaplains must be allowed to make their own decisions regarding standing up for what's right. If other chaplains do not have the guts to stand up against those things that are wrong, that's their problem. There are times when I definitely don't agree with what has happened or is happening among the chaplains, but we have to stand, even if it means standing by oneself! Don't throw out the baby with the bath water. I have good friends in many religious faith groups that are chaplains/clergymen. I respect them; they show me respect. But, that does not affect the facts in the least.

Another problem within the ranks of the chaplaincy is that there are some chaplains representing certain denominations who go to any means to reach the top and, once they are in a top leadership position such as Command Chaplain, ninety percent of the time he will not approve or recommend promotion for a chaplain of another denomination, especially if the other chaplains have leadership potential. Why is it this way? We can argue the point until we become blue in the face, but it will not change the facts. Chaplains representing full-gospel denominations are held back when it comes to supervisory chaplain positions.

Also, I must state that I have been disappointed with the actions and outright deliberate attempts by some senior chaplains or commanders to destroy the character of certain chaplains. But I feel pity for them more than anything else. It is very important for me at this time to say very forcefully that all senior chaplains or commanders are not bad leaders; neither are subordinate chaplains, there are just a few that operate negatively and smell up the others!

However, there are exceptions to this rule, thank the Lord. You probably would ask me, "How do you know this is fact?" I am glad you asked the question. I know from personal experience. I have been involved with and I have had to deal with this subject personally. Also, I know from previous conversations with another chaplain now serving on active duty. He had to go through similar discrimination. And, there are probably many other chaplains that have experienced this type of discrimination.

Another reason that I can answer this question in a positive manner results from what I have heard personally from individuals who were in command positions. These individuals let their mouths get in gear before their minds did. I witnessed this myself, by accident. I came upon a conversation between a senior officer and a chaplain discussing this very subject, full gospel chaplains. Both men were blasting a chaplain's reputation because he spoke out against unethical and sinful practices by chaplains and officers, and the chaplain they were roasting was not from my denomination . . . he was just a good old Southern Baptist. I was seated in a booth next to them and they did not even know I was nearby. That was one time I just kept quiet . . . which was hard for me to do! You learn a lot by keeping quiet sometimes. It is one thing to hear it from someone not in a command position, but to hear it stated by an individual holding a command position is discouraging, to say the least. And, to top it all off—the negative conversation involved another chaplain . . . trying to make points!

When men and women of God, individuals performing duties as chaplains, cannot work together without being prejudiced toward another person's religious faith group, that's sad! How can a chaplain, a representative of God, honestly help someone with a problem, when there are more serious problems existing in their own lives? I know this is not an easy subject to discuss, but nevertheless, the barrier must be broken down. Chaplains must become responsible for their behavior.

Now don't you think for a minute this problem will go away. It will not. It will continue. However, you and I must take charge of our lives and *stop* it at this point! *The buck stops here*! God, our commander, is looking on! He has the last word!

3. Discrimination Against A Religious Faith

Once upon a time there were three chaplains serving in a state militia; one was the Command Chaplain and the other two were his subordinate chaplains. We will call the subordinate chaplains Chaplain #1 and Chaplain #2. Two of the chaplains, the Command Chaplain and Chaplain #2, were from religious faith groups other than a full gospel faith group, while Chaplain #1 was from a "holiness" denomination. The Command Chaplain was senior in time and grade. Chaplain #1 was next to him in seniority; the other chaplain, Chaplain #2, was a year shorter in time and grade than Chaplain #1. However, the buddy system was in the works.

The Command Chaplain was going to promote Chaplain #2 over Chaplain #1 without giving Chaplain #1 due consideration or be informed that a promotion was being considered for one of the chaplains directly under his command. This was being done in a backroom conference between the Command Chaplain and Chaplain #2. Plus, it was a known fact that Chaplain #2's performance was sub-par, and his attendance and production less than satisfactory. He should have been discharged long ago. But, a promotion was coming! Chaplain #1 heard about the backroom conference and the premeditated plans. Dare to say, it did not sit well with him at all. When Chaplain #1 heard about the proposed planned promotion for Chaplain #2, and that Chaplain #2 was to become his superior, it frustrated him highly. Chaplain #1's holy indignation rose up in him. However, he was aware of his anger level, and he concentrated on defeating the "devilish spirit" and trying *not* to sin. "Anger and sin not" rang out as a spiritual warning!

Chaplain #1's approach was to get an appointment with the Command Chaplain and discuss this personnel matter face-to-face. Arrangements were made. However, the Command Chaplain was not aware of Chaplain #1's knowledge of his planned promotion for Chaplain #2. Their meeting was held in a closed-door setting. Chaplain #1 immediately informed the Command Chaplain of what he had heard unofficially, but expressed that he believed it was probably somewhat true. The Command Chaplain's reaction gave the impression that he understood where Chaplain #1 was coming from, but seemed a little surprised that he knew so much about it. Chaplain #1 stated that he could have called him on the telephone and discussed his concern, or he could have written him a letter, but he preferred to talk to him face-to-face.

Chaplain #1 had a copy of his 201 file (personnel record) and began a verbal review of it. Chaplain #1 explained that his chaplain experience and the annual evaluations completed by him (Command Chaplain) were rated as outstanding. Also, his educational background and training record were equal to that of the Command Chaplain, except that the Command Chaplain had a doctorate and Chaplain #1 did not. He only had a M.A. degree.

Chaplain #1 and Chaplain #2 had equal education. Chaplain #1's attendance record was exceptional and Chaplain #2's record was marginal. Chaplain #1's work production was above average. Chaplain #2's record was marginal-to-unsatisfactory. Plus, during the Command Chaplain's time-off duty for personal reasons, Chaplain #1 supervised the chaplain branch in his absence in an above average manner, while Chaplain #2's involvement was marginal.

Finally, Chaplain #1 informed the Command Chaplain that he had compared his total record and the total record of Chaplain #2. The only thing he had not been able to rule out, that evidently had something to do with him being passed over, was the question concerning his religious faith and his ministerial credentials coming from a full gospel church, a holiness denomination. Chaplain #1 then asked the Command Chaplain the question, "Are you prejudiced against me because of my religious faith or being from a holiness denomination?" Chaplain #1 waited for an answer from the Command Chaplain. It was slow coming out! Facial expressions, eye movement and body language all are indicators to Chaplain #1 that there was a "rat in the wood pile," and that he had hit a "home run question."

Chaplain #1 stated to the Command Chaplain while he was "thinking," as an illustrated point, that his grandpa once said to him, "When you talk to a person, always observe the individual by following the person's eyes. The eyes will reveal a lot about the person. If the individual will not look you in the eye, it reveals a negative sign of not being truthful. So, target the eyes, the eyes are the windows to the soul." Chaplain #1 also stated that he had followed his grandpa's instructions more than once, and it seemed to work every time. And, it worked this time, as well.

To allow more time to think about how to respond to Chaplain #1's question, the Command Chaplain parroted the question a couple of times. Finally the Command Chaplain stated that he was not prejudice against him because of his religious faith, especially because he came from a "holiness" background.

Chaplain #1 then replied, "I will take you at your word, because you are a minister and chaplain. However, as a result of our meeting and your response, I do not expect to have any more problems with this subject." They shook hands, and Chaplain #1 departed . . . still skeptical.

About three months afterwards, Chaplain #1 and Chaplain #2 both were promoted to 05. Within the next eighteen to twenty-four months, Chaplain #2 had a serious heart attack; he later died from complications.

Note: Chaplain #2 never became aware of the meeting conducted between the Command Chaplain and Chaplain #1; therefore, it had nothing to do with Chaplain #2's heart attack.

Now to show you that the Lord does not love ugliness, things began to happen. Changes began to be made. The Command Chaplain was moved from his Command Chaplain position to Special Assistant to the Commander, and Chaplain #1 was appointed "Acting Command Chaplain."

About six months later, Chaplain #1 was appointed as the Command Chaplain and promoted to 06. There is more to tell about this scenario, but this is a good stopping place.

Nevertheless, the story has another part to it that could serve very adequately to support the fact that some clergy or chaplains hunger for power. They will go to whatever means to obtain their objective. That hunger feeds the ego and cultivates prejudicial acts that destroy everything good in its path. A warning—do not do evil things just to get ahead!

Any type of promotion or advancement one receives at the expense of another through a premeditated act for self-gain will one day boomerang, *not* to speak of how the Lord will react to the conspiracy. Judas was *not* the only betrayer!

Note: Names and places were omitted to protect all parties!

Do not practice deceit! When one uses premeditated acts of betrayal, there is danger ahead. Christian people have been attacked more from within than from outside. This example supports the "Trojan Horse Theory"—It's not what is showing on the outside of a person that is harmful; it's what is not seen on the inside of a person that is dangerous.

4. Disrespect

Our country's colony-by-colony protection was established by utilizing the "home guard" as a military militia. The first president of the United States, George Washington himself, volunteered and served in the home guard, the Virginia Militia. And, all throughout history volunteerism has prevailed in a positive manner, at no cost. If this is true, and it is factual history, then *why* would an official paid military group treat the volunteers so disrespectful? Maybe it's because they get paid, and patriotic volunteers do the same job, and do it better sometimes . . . without pay, or, it may be something else . . . jealousy.

First of all the volunteer military unit must be under the command of the State's Adjutant General and trained to function militarily, otherwise he/she cannot become a member. Those selected to serve in leadership must be qualified and trained to command. Second, the assigned tasks come down from the Adjutant General and are evaluated annually. Third, the volunteers serve and perform their military duties and responsibilities at no cost to the state. You cannot beat that price! Fourth, the volunteer state military unit serves as a backup to the National Guard, subject to state duty call up when and if the National Guard is federalized. The state must not be left without a viable military unit to perform duties when and if call up by the Governor is requested by the Adjutant General (pay for performance and/or food/travel would be initiated once officially called to duty).

So, why would the State Guard members be treated disrespectfully by the National Guard line officers and NCO's (treated like red-headed, adopted step-children)? It has been done in many cases, and still to my knowledge it goes on . . . against chaplains as well as other members. Ignorance is no excuse!

Even religious denominations practice disrespect unjustifiably against their members that serve as volunteers in the State Guard or Civil Air Patrol. I have observed it and have experienced it, too. However, when I hear about it I do a personal "witch hunt" on those person(s) that have been guilty of expressing their thoughts out loud, but not in the presence of the individuals they are talking about. I find in many cases that the individual(s) making disrespectful remarks could not qualify to serve themselves in a position equal to the one they are gossiping about, because of lack of education and/or expertise. So sad!

Unethical Practices Against Chaplains

It is unbelievable that a commander would not want to have a chaplain on his personal staff, but it has happened and will continue to be a hidden agenda of some commanders that practice unethical behavior. It is also a known fact that some chaplains practice unethical behavior: alcoholism, drug addiction, domestic abuse, homosexuality, and the list goes on. It is also a known fact that chaplains or clergy, and it's safe to say, no Christian, does these type of things unless he/she has fallen away from the faith. It's very clear that when a person commits sin, he/she becomes a sinner, and must repent to be restored to the fellowship of the Lord. These are God's rules, not mine!

It is also unbelievable why a chaplain so driven to be promoted or to be assigned to an important leadership position that he/she would stoop to such low morals to use behind-the-scenes tactics to receive favor from superiors and/or other chaplains that may have clout for the sole purpose of moving ahead of a more deserving chaplain, senior in time and grade, just to be able to wear the rank and hold the title. So sad. But, God knows! If you don't treat people good/fair on the way up, you'll pass 'em on the way down.

Also, if you are going in a direction and came up on the devil going in the same direction, you are going the wrong way. The devil does not go in the same direction as the righteous!

The examples used in this section are primarily used in a way to give you a wide open field of mannerism and attitudes that could possibly happen. You alone will have to judge if the behaviors were right or wrong. These examples are possibly, for lack of a better word, fictional in content, but what if they were true? How would you react? What would you do if it happened to you? Or, maybe some of this has happened to you or by you during your lifetime. If you are one of the characters doing an unethical thing, and you don't straighten it up before your death, you will have a high cross bar to jump over at the entrance into Heaven. Like the famous Paul Harvey said, "You know the rest of the story."

You have the choice of believing the gospel or not believing it . . . I have no problem with believing its Word! Our individual cases will be heard and judged by Almighty God. The jury is out!

✝

Chapter Eleven:

COMMAND CHAPLAIN PERFORMANCE AND MASTER RELIGIOUS CURRICULUM

The Performance Plan for Chaplains

The Command Chaplain Performance Plan and Master Religious Curriculum (CCPP and MRC) arc structured as a guideline to identify specific procedures, training, assistance and services that the Command Chaplain must provide to subordinate chaplains for implementing as chaplain services to the military family as guaranteed under the First Amendment of the United States Constitution, the right to the free expression of religion.

Therefore, the CCPP and MRC will provide an agenda for the Command Chaplain to follow in training subordinate chaplains to carry out the directives of superiors, without deviation from the religious beliefs of the individuals, including those of the Command Chaplain and/or subordinate chaplains.[19]

The U.S. Code, Title 10 and military regulations provide specific guidelines for chaplains to follow, and require commanders to provide for the religious needs of military personnel. The Command Chaplain will prepare a standard operating procedure, coordinate classes of instructions, provide religious program supervision to all subordinate chaplains, and establish a communication and reporting system for chaplains to follow in compliance with the chain of command (both in the office of their immediate commander and the office of the Command Chaplain).

The subordinate chaplains will be required to prepare a Chaplain Performance Plan and Religious Curriculum (CPP and RC) for their assigned command by incorporating the goals and objectives of the Command Chaplain set out in the CCPP and MRC.

This will provide uniformity in carrying out the chaplain's duties, and at the same time it will have a built-in tool for measuring and evaluating the success or failure of the chaplain's support to the commander. It also insures compliance to the First Amendment of the U.S. Constitution, because it provides every soldier with access to a chaplain of their religious faith group.

The religious rights guaranteed in the First Amendment of the U.S. Constitution are exercised by individuals when they do not present a problem while a military mission is being carried out. In other words, all soldiers, when it does not jeopardize the military mission, will be allowed to practice their religious worship according to their faith, observe holy days, practice the dietary laws of their faith, participate in rites, sacraments and ordinances, receive medical treatment according to their religious faith, and be allowed to wear religious garments and maintain religious appearance requirements.

The Command Chaplain Performance Plan and Master Religious Program will be prepared by the Command Chaplain/Chief of Chaplains, and delegated to his subordinate chaplains to review and incorporate into a prepared Performance Plan and the Chaplain Religious Program on their level of command.

The plans and programs are coordinated to function as a structured guideline to provide identified needs and services that will be useable for the chaplain in performing the assigned chaplain tasks. The plan and program will provide a means to:

- carry out realistic goals and objectives,
- plan an appropriate religious military ministry for the personnel within his or her command,
- prepare an annual functional budget to support the chaplain ministry, and
- provide a method to annually evaluate the religious program by utilizing an ongoing review and revision process to keep the chaplain ministry productive, professional and militarily providing direct ministry to the officers, enlisted personnel and their families.

Specific Guidelines

The Command Chaplain/Chief of Chaplains will plan the annual Command Chaplain Performance Plan and Master Religious Program (CCPP and MRP), and distribute it to his subordinate chaplains throughout the command.

Each subordinate chaplain:

- will be responsible for reviewing and complying with the plan and program directed by the Command Chaplain/Chief of Chaplains,

- must prepare an annual Chaplain Performance Plan and Religious Program (CPP and RP), incorporating into their plan and program the goals and objectives published by the Command Chaplain/Chief of Chaplains, and
- will discuss the CPP and RP with the chaplain's commander through a thorough orientation, and receive the commander's approval of the religious plan and religious program to be operational within the command.

This instructional material has been written in understandable language, and is to be utilized as a guide for the volunteer chaplain. It stresses the responsibilities that the command chaplain and the subordinate chaplain have delegated for providing:

- chaplain services for the command's personnel,
- support to the commander as the commander's religious advisor, and
- subordination to the Command Chaplain/Chief of Chaplains for maintaining the ethical standards of behavior required of a chaplain.

The Role of the Chaplain

- The chaplain must always take the leadership in planning and providing religious services.
- When religious services have been finalized and approval has been given, the chaplain must communicate and distribute the scheduling to the commander and subordinate staff, with a copy distributed to the Chief of Chaplains.
- The scheduling of religious services should be planned in such a precise manner that it does not compete with the command's operation functions.

- It is very important that the chaplain place priority on establishing and maintaining a working relationship with the commander and his staff, always recognizing and respecting the responsibility of the commander.
- The command personnel have the option to participate or not to participate in religious services.
- No chaplain will be required to conduct any religious service or rite that is contrary to the regulation or tenets of his/her denomination.
- Neither can a chaplain be required or commanded to officiate jointly in a religious service with a chaplain or a member of the civilian clergy of another denomination.

Chaplain Involvement

- The Chief of Chaplains is a member of the Commanding General's staff, and the subordinate chaplain is a member of his/her commander's staff.
- The chaplains respectfully address their commander on behalf of all chaplains and chaplain assistants on matters pertaining to religion, morals, and morale as deemed necessary.
- Communication between the volunteer chaplain and the Commander and his Chief of Staff or senior subordinate must be established and maintained, regardless of personality conflict.
- The position of the commander must be respected.
- The chaplain must establish communication with his/her commander, no matter what level of command he/she is assigned.
- The chaplain must establish a distribution list and properly distribute information through the chain of command.

Dual-Role Functions

The subordinate chaplain performs the following chaplain duties and responsibilities under a dual supervisory role:

- The commander must be informed of the chaplain's business responses in complying to directives received from the Command Chaplain.
- Subordinate chaplains are held accountable to the Command Chaplain/Chief of Chaplains for:
- designated reporting,
- attending scheduled chaplain training, and
- maintaining the ethical standards of behavior required of a chaplain.

The plan and program will provide a uniform manner in which each chaplain will perform the duties and responsibilities required of a chaplain, such as,

- providing training material for the chaplain and staff to serve effectively and to accomplish assigned tasks,
- providing ministry direction in responding to mobilization and deployment,
- encouraging absolute faithful and loyal support to the command's mission,
- performing duties and responsibilities in an ethical, professional and honorable manner, and
- providing a ministry of dedicated service to the com-mand's personnel and their families for a better quality of life.

Teamwork Approach

The chaplain "teamwork approach" will enhance the overall effectiveness in meeting the command's spiritual, moral and morale needs.

The teamwork approach is characterized by:
- compliance with the Command Chaplains/Chief of Chaplain's CCPP and MRP,
- planning the chaplain's CPP and RP,
- setting realistic goals and objectives that are measurable annually,
- planning an appropriate religious ministry program to meet the needs all military personnel of the command;
- exploring the possibility of establishing a chaplain fund, accompanied by an annual budget, to support the chaplain ministry (this must be submitted in writing to the commander and the Command Chaplain/ Chief of Chaplains for approval prior to implementation).
- planning a mobilization strategy,
- planning a recruiting campaign, and
- establishing a plan to communicate with the religious organizations in the community.

Chaplain Assistance

The Chaplain will be responsible for:
- providing training material for the chaplain and chaplain assistant in preparation to serve effectively and to accomplish assigned tasks,
- providing ministry direction in responding to mobilization and deployment,
- encouraging absolute faithful and loyal support to the command's mission,
- performing chaplain duties and responsibilities in an ethical, professional, and honorable manner, and
- providing a ministry of dedicated service to the command's personnel for a better quality of life for every one.

Mission and Mobilization

- Plan, coordinate and train for mobilization and deployment.
- Support the mission and its personnel.
- Provide professional development opportunities for chaplain assistants and command staff.
- Plan, acquire and manage responsibly all entrusted resources.
- Participate with community civic and religious leaders as a responsible partner by planning objectively for future needs.
- Plan and prepare to perform requests for military funerals.

General Chaplain Functions

- Advise the commander and his staff on religion, morals and morale as it may be affected by religion.
- Plan and supervise the assigned budget (provided a budget is assigned).
- Organize, plan and supervise all religious services, chaplain functions and activities.
- Provide religious services, pastoral care and counseling for command personnel and their families, and other authorized persons.
- Supervisory chaplains: review, evaluate and submit recommendations for the assignment of chaplains and chaplain assistants.
- Supervise and monitor the use, maintenance and replacement of chaplains' religious supplies, equipment and facilities.
- Plan, develop, coordinate and supervise meetings, workshops/seminars and training programs scheduled for chaplains and chaplain assistants.

- Conduct training classes on moral leadership and other requested subjects when recommended by the commander or subordinate commanders.
- Establish and maintain a working relationship with chaplains serving in the active military, subordinate commands, religious leaders, and civilian community organizations.
- Provide reports on personal religious activities, utilization of chaplains and chaplain assistants for military funerals, training exercises, mobilization and other contingency plans.
- Perform any other chaplain-related duties as directed.
- The scheduling of religious services should be planned in such a precise manner that it does not compete with the command's operation functions.
- It is very important that the chaplain place priority on establishing and maintaining a working relationship with the commander and his staff, always recognizing and respecting the responsibility of the commander.
- The command personnel have the option to participate or not to participate in religious services.
- No chaplain will be required to conduct any religious service or rite that is contrary to the regulation or tenets of his/her denomination.
- Neither can a chaplain be required or commanded to officiate jointly in a religious service with a chaplain or a member of the civilian clergy of another denomination.[20]

General Religious Services

- There are times when a general religious service can be scheduled.
- Keep in mind that a general religious service is not a Protestant, Catholic or Jewish service. It will include only those elements that are common to all faiths.

- The general service will not embarrass any person, and will make it possible for participants to assist in a general worship service that is meaningful to each person.
- A general religious service may include, but is not limited to the following elements:
  - ❖ Recognition of the presence of God.
  - ❖ A time for silent prayer.
  - ❖ Reading from the Old Testament (especially the Psalms).
  - ❖ General expressions of sorrow for the lack of charity toward others.
  - ❖ Petitions of God's blessings for civil authorities.
  - ❖ A thanksgiving for shared blessings.
- A prior understanding and even an explanation of the nature of a general religious service will be helpful, and may even be necessary to eliminate doubts or disturbing surprises.
- The chaplain should be aware of, and sensitive to, the needs of faith groups. The recognition of ethnic backgrounds and customs will enhance general religious services.

Protocol

- Communication between the volunteer chaplain and the Commander and his Chief of Staff or senior subordinate must be established and maintained, regardless of personality conflict.
- The position of the commander must be respected.
- The chaplain must establish communication with his/her commander, no matter what level of command he/she is assigned.
- The chaplain must establish a distribution list and properly distribute information through the chain of command.

Personnel Utilization
- Provide procedures to be followed by the chaplain when command personnel are being assigned to participate in an approved religious or command mission or task, such as:
  - mobilization and deployment response (disaster preparedness),
  - military funerals,
  - chaplain continuing education,
  - training for chaplain assistants and staff, and
  - other transfers and/or assignments.

Chaplain and Chaplain Assistant Annual Evaluation

Annually an evaluation of the chaplain and the chaplain's staff will be conducted. The Command Chaplain/ Chief of Chaplains will:
- Provide a uniform annual evaluation form.
- Set date and time for the evaluation.
- Schedule a training class on evaluation procedures and require all chaplains to attend.
- Evaluate subordinate supervisory chaplains.
- Be evaluated by the immediate commander or designee.
- Review annually or as necessary the subordinate's record for promotions and/or awards.

✝

Chapter Twelve:

ESTABLISHING COMMAND GOALS AND OBJECTIVES

Realistic and Measurable
- The Chief of Chaplains will plan, coordinate, and train his subordinate chaplain staff on the importance of establishing annual goals and objectives.
- It will provide factual data to fairly and impartially consider chaplains and their staff for promotion, including recognizing chaplains and their staff for awards, et cetera.

Mobilization and Deployment
- Provide chaplains and chaplain staff assistance to commanders when official orders have been issued to his command for mobilization and deployment of command personnel.
- Mobilization and deployment training will be conducted by the commander or his designee. All chaplains and their staff will attend the training and participate in all scheduled mobilization and deployment orientation.

Training for Mobilization
- Chaplains will participate in all mobilization and deployment training/planning classes scheduled/conducted by the commander or his designee.

- The chaplain will become familiar with the chaplain's role during mobilization and deployment.
- The chaplain will maintain a state of readiness in support of the disaster preparedness mobilization and deployment response.

Military Funerals

- Chaplains and chaplain staff must provide assistance to the commander, the county service officer, the funeral director, the family of the deceased military person or veteran, and other recognized officials when a message has been received requesting for military funeral detail
- The Command Chaplain/Chief of Chaplains will plan,coordinate and require all chaplains to attend training classes on military funerals.
- No chaplain will conduct a military funeral until military funeral training has been completed.
- All military funerals will be conducted in Class A uniforms, unless otherwise directed.
- It is strongly recommended that a chaplain assist another experienced chaplain with a military funeral before one is conducted alone.
- This is the last respect and honor that can be shown to a deceased veteran; it must be conducted without any mistakes.

Selection of Goals and Objectives

- Command Chaplain/Chief of Chaplains will counsel with each subordinate chaplain and staff member concerning job performance and the importance of establishing annual measurable short-range and long-range goals and objectives.
- Each member on the staff of the Command Chaplain/ Chief of Chaplains will be required to choose a min-

imum of five goals and objectives to be accomplished over the upcoming year.

- Once these goals and objectives have been decided upon by the subordinate chaplain/staff member, a joint review will be scheduled.
- Annually the Command Chaplain/Chief of Chaplains will require the subordinate chaplains and their staff to perform an annual review of the goals and objectives each of them have made previously. The review will be documented in writing (report format) by each chaplain and staff member, and forwarded to the Command Chaplain/Chief of Chaplains for review and comments.
- Once the Command Chaplain/Chief of Chaplains has reviewed the subordinate chaplain and staff member's submitted report, a scheduled joint review will be planned and conducted.

Sample: Goal #1

The chaplain will assist and support the commander when official orders have been issued to his command for mobilization and deployment of command personnel.

Objectives and Tasks:

- The chaplain will attend the Mission Orientation and meet with the commander and the command staff at a time and place designated by the commander, and receive information at the mission orientation.
- The chaplain will request and discuss the chaplain's role with the commander; once the role is defined, the chaplain will function as a part of the mobilization and deployment team.
- All chaplains that become involved in the mobilization and deployment call-up, and come from outside

of the command mission area, will be subordinate to the designated chaplain-in-charge.

- All chaplain functions will be worked through that designated mission chaplain.
- Every chaplain assigned to the mission task will complete an After Action Report outlining their chaplain duties/performance.
- The After Action Report will be distributed to the mission task commander or designee; copies will be distributed to the up line chain of command.

Complete:

The chaplain will construct a sample commander's call-up order and write up the details of what occurs at the meeting(s) of a commander's mobilization and deployment plan. The chaplain will also complete an After Action Report, giving details of what happened, et cetera.

Sample: Goal #2

The chaplain will provide assistance to the commander, the county service officer, the funeral director and other recognized officials when a request is made for a military funeral detail.

Objectives and Tasks:

The chaplain will:

- Assist the commander, the funeral director, the county service officer or other recognized officials when a request is received requesting assistance in conducting a military funeral.
- Plan and coordinate with the funeral director to obtain a U.S. flag from the county service officer or U.S. Post Office (do this only if you are requested to assist).

- *Note*: If active duty military personnel cannot be acquired, the chaplain will assist the funeral director in recruiting command personnel to act as pallbearers by:
- Requesting military personnel assistance through the commander (the commander will be responsible for recruiting the funeral personnel from among his command and placing them on official orders, or the chaplain will assist, if requested by the commander).
- When the military funeral detail has been finalized, and the time and place have been coordinated with all personnel, the chaplain will meet with the funeral detail prior to the funeral to review the procedures to be followed.
- The chaplain will complete an After Action Report and submit copies of the report to the commander with copies distributed up through the chain of command.

Complete:
An After Action Report/Funeral Report.

Sample: Goal #3
Other chaplain-related duties and responsibilities that will be performed to support the commander and the command personnel include retention, recruiting, military funerals, and performing other duties, as directed.

Objectives and Tasks:
Retention/Recruitment:
- The Chief of Chaplains/Chaplain will conduct a staff study to possibly create a policy for retention, recruitment and programs, and submit it to the commander for approval consideration.

- If the policy is approved the chaplain position will be coordinated through channels, and the appointment of a chaplain to serve in that position will be finalized.
- The retention, recruitment and programs chaplain will work with the commander's staff chaplain on absenteeism, and devise a plan of action to follow up on absentees and to reduce the number of drop-outs/discharges.
- In the event the command member has an accident, or, if there is a death, the command can become aware of the problem within a reasonable period of time, thus being available to offer support to the command member and/or their family.

Note: Implementation of a Personal Information Card (PIC) to be filled out by the chaplain on all command personnel, and used for follow-up purposes.

Military Funeral Coordinator

The Chief of Chaplains will submit to his commander a request recommending an additional chaplain position, Military Funeral Coordinator. If approved, a chaplain will be appointed to serve.

Duties:

Coordinating requests for military funerals and maintaining a record system.

✝

Chapter Thirteen:

SAMPLE JOB DESCRIPTIONS

Job descriptions for all chaplain staff are a must. There should be a clear and precise job description in printed form. The information should be distributed to each staff member, followed up by a personal counseling session to give direction to all chaplains and chaplain staff. Not only will it provide a method for staff to be evaluated for specific assignments to leadership/supervisory positions, but it will provide accurate data for recognizing deserving staff for awards and/or promotions.

Command Chaplain/Chief of Chaplains

The Command Chaplain/Chief of Chaplains will:
I.   Plan, supervise and coordinate religious activities for all chaplains assigned to the headquarters and subordinate commands.
II. Provide chaplain support to all chaplains in subordinate commands.
III. Perform chaplain services and coverage where and when needed.
IV. Perform specific duties and responsibilities, and any other command directives necessary to carry out the command mission.
V.   Advise the Commanding General and his subordinate staff on all matters pertaining to religion,

morality, and morale that may be affected by religion and the assignment of chaplains within the command.

VI. Be prepared, when called upon by the Commanding General and his subordinate staff to:
- provide constructive counseling,
- provide leadership in the planning and developing of a religious program directed toward improving the moral and ethical quality of life for command personnel,
- provide biblical self-development, and
- provide problem solving for subordinate chaplains, chaplain assistants and command personnel.

VII. Recommend to the commander ways and methods to present chaplain activities to the general public.

VIII. Provide supervision of all assigned equipment and supplies, and maintain a recordkeeping system of accountability.

IX. Submit approval requests to the commander for special activities and other programs not provided by the unit assigned chaplain.

X. Advise the commander and his subordinate staff of emerging and unfamiliar religious groups with the command.

XI. Perform periodic evaluation of the spiritual and moral health of all the commands, to include an evaluation of the ethical and biblical depth of the command policies, leadership practices and supervision styles.

XII. Organize, plan and semiannually conduct a chaplain training conference/workshop for all chaplains and chaplain assistants.

XIII. Establish and maintain liaison with chaplains of higher and subordinate commands, other branches of military services, government agencies, and officials of civilian church organizations.

XIV. Integrate chapel activities into the overall program of the command.

XV. Institute an extensive and continuous religious program to encourage chaplain and chaplain assistant's retention and recruitment.

XVI. Monitor and submit recommendations to the Commanding General of concerns related to chaplain equipment, facilities and reclassification of staff positions.

XVII. Visit subordinate brigade, battalion and companies annually, if practically possible.

XVIII. Plan and conduct a chaplain's training conference/workshop for all chaplains and chaplain assistants at least semiannually and/or as required.

XIX. Audit all chaplain funds and chaplain records at least annually.

XX. Attend all scheduled chaplain and Chief of Staff meetings as directed.

XXI. Complete the Basic Officers' Course during first membership year.

XXII. Attend a minimum of eighty percent of all scheduled monthly meetings to maintain satisfactory attendance record.

XXIII. Perform other duties as directed by the commander.

Deputy Command Chaplain/Chief of Chaplains

The Deputy Command Chaplain/Deputy Chief of Chaplains will:

I. Assist the Command Chaplain/Chief of Chaplains with planning, supervising and coordinating the chaplain religious activities for all chaplains assigned to the headquarters and subordinate commands.

II. Prepare a plan of action to provide specific support to all chaplains assigned to the headquarters and subordinate commands.

III. Prepare and keep a current listing of all chaplain positions and the name of the chaplain assigned to that position, and when there is a chaplain vacancy throughout the command, coordinate chaplain services and coverage where and when needed (provide the Command chaplain/Chief of Chaplains with an updated roster monthly).

IV. Perform specific duties and responsibilities, and any other command directives necessary to carry out the command mission.

V. In the absence of the Command Chaplain/Chief of Chaplains, be prepared to advise the Commanding General and his staff on all matters pertaining to religion, morality, and morale that may be affected by religion and the use of chaplains within the command.

VI. When directed by the Command Chaplain/Chief of Chaplains, be prepared when called upon by the Commanding General and his staff to:
- give constructive counseling,
- provide leadership in planning and developing a religious program directed toward improving the moral and ethical quality of life for command personnel, and
- recommend ways and methods to present chaplain activities to the general public.

VII. Supervise the use and upkeep of assigned and authorized equipment.

VIII. Request approval for special activities and other programs not provided by the unit assigned chaplain.

IX. Advise the Command Chaplain/Chief of Chaplains, the commander, and his subordinate staff on emerging and unfamiliar religious groups within the command.

X. Perform periodic evaluation of the spiritual and moral health of all the commands, to include an evaluation of the ethical and biblical depth of the command policies, leadership practices and supervision styles.

XI. Assist the Command Chaplain/Chief of Chaplain in planning and supervising the chaplain and chaplain assistant training.

XII. Establish and maintain liaison with chaplains of higher and subordinate commands, other branches of military services, government agencies, and officials of church organizations.

XIII. Integrate chapel activities into the overall program of the command.

XIV. Monitor and submit recommendations to the Command Chaplain/Chief of Chaplains of concerns related to equipment, facilities and reclassification and revisions of staff positions.

XV. Visit subordinate commands, as directed, especially during scheduled training.

XVI. Assist in planning and conducting chaplain's training conference/workshop for all chaplains and chaplain assistants at least semiannually and/or as required.

XVII. Assist in auditing all chaplain funds and chaplain records at least annually.

XVIII. Attend all scheduled chaplain staff meetings, as directed.

XIX. Complete the Basic Officers' Course during first membership year.

XX. Attend a minimum of eighty percent of all scheduled monthly meetings to maintain a satisfactory attendance report.

XXI. Perform other duties as directed by the Command Chaplain/Chief of Chaplains and/or the commander.

Brigade Chaplain

The Brigade Chaplain will:

I. Perform specific chaplain duties, responsibilities and any other command directives necessary to assist in carrying out the brigade mission.

- Advise the Brigade Commander and his subordinate staff on all matters pertaining to religion, morality, and morale that may be affected by religion and the use of chaplains within the command.
- Be prepared to respond to requests from the commander and his subordinate staff to:
  * provide constructive counseling,
  * provide leadership in planning and developing a religious program directed toward assisting the moral and ethical quality of the brigade personnel, provide biblical self-development, and provide problems solving services.
- Advise the commander on emerging and unfamiliar religious groups within the brigade.
- Perform the annual evaluation of the brigade chaplains' and chaplain assistants' performance and religious training.
- Integrate chapel services and religious activities throughout the command.
- Provide equipment and supplies for chaplains.

II. Prepare a chaplain support plan for subordinate brigade chaplains to respond to mobilization and deployment during an emergency call-out;

III. Coordinate all requests for military funeral details with subordinate chaplains and brigade personnel.

- Provide military funeral training for all subordinate chaplains and chaplain assistants throughout the brigade command.
- IV. Attend scheduled chaplain staff meetings as directed.
- V. Complete the Basic Officers' Course during the first membership year.
- VI. Attend a minimum of eighty percent of all scheduled monthly meetings to maintain a satisfactory attendance record.
- VII. Prepare and submit all quarterly chaplain reports to the commander, with copies forwarded to the Command Chaplain/Chief of Chaplains.
- VIII. Perform other duties as directed.

Battalion Chaplain

The Battalion Chaplain will:

- I. Perform specific chaplain duties, responsibilities and any other command directives necessary to assist in carrying out the battalion mission.
  - Advise the Battalion Commander and his subordinate staff on all matters pertaining to religion, moral, and morale that may be affected by religion and the use of chaplains within the command.
  - Be prepared to respond to requests from the commander and his subordinate staff to:
    - ❖ provide constructive counseling,
    - ❖ provide leadership in planning and developing a religious program directed toward assisting the moraland ethical quality of the battalion personnel,
    - ❖ provide biblical self-development, and
    - ❖ provide problem-solving services.
  - Advise the command on emerging and unfamiliar religious groups within the brigade.

- Perform the annual evaluation of the battalion chaplain assistants' performance and religious training.
- Integrate chapel services and religious activities throughout the battalion command.
- Provide equipment and supplies for chaplain assistants.

II. Prepare a chaplain assistant support plan for subordinate chaplain assistants to respond to mobilization and deployment during an emergency call-out.

III. Coordinate with the battalion commander all incoming requests for military funerals.
   - Provide military funeral training for all chaplain assistants and command personnel throughout the battalion command.

IV. Attend scheduled chaplain staff meetings as directed.

V. Complete the Basic Officers' Course during the first membership year.

VI. Attend a minimum of eighty percent of all scheduled monthly meeting to maintain a satisfactory attendance record.

VII. Prepare and submit all quarterly chaplain reports to the commander, with copies forwarded to the Brigade Chaplain.

VIII. Perform other duties as directed.

Deputy Staff Chaplain for Administration

The Deputy Staff Chaplain for Administration will:

I. Be responsible for maintaining all Chaplain Section record files.

II. Plan, supervise and coordinate the management of all chaplain reports by compiling data from the reports into a consolidated report to be presented to the Chief of Staff.

   III. Plan, develop and establish a record keeping system for assignment and issuance of all equipment and supplies to assigned chaplain staff personnel.

   IV. Prepare and keep a current listing of all chaplain positions, the name of the chaplain assigned to that position, current address/telephone information, and maintain a current recordkeeping system.

   V. Prepare all official requests for orders, awards, promotion and scheduled religious activities;

   VI. Establish a file record on state guard staff, local military commands, government agencies, religious organizations, and other information as directed.

   VII. Prepare transfers in and out.

   VIII. Attend scheduled chaplain staff meetings as directed.

   IX. Complete the Basic Officers' Course during the first membership year.

   X. Attend a minimum of eighty percent of all scheduled monthly meetings to maintain a satisfactory attendance record.

   XI. Prepare and submit all quarterly chaplain reports, and other reports, as directed.

   XII. Perform other duties as directed by the Command Chaplain/Chief of Chaplains and other superiors.

Chaplain Assistant (E-5) — (HDD/HCC)

The Chaplain Assistant will:

   I. Perform chaplain assistant duties, responsibilities and any other command directives necessary to assist in carrying out the command mission.

   II. Advise the chaplain on all matters pertaining to religion, morality, and morale that may be affected by religion within the command;

   III. Advise the chaplain of unfamiliar religious groups within the command.

IV. Assist in integrating chapel services and religious activities throughout the command.

V. Maintain an inventory of chaplain equipment and supplies, and a recordkeeping system.

VI. Assist the chaplain in preparing a chaplain support plan for chaplain assistance to respond to mobilization and deployment during an emergency call-out.

VII. Assist the chaplain and command personnel with all incoming requests for military funerals.

VIII. Assist the chaplain in planning/conducting military funeral training for all subordinate chaplain assistants and command personnel through out the command;

IX. Perform administrative duties and responsibilities by:
  • maintaining administrative records and clerical duties,
  • providing administrative office management,
  • keeping updated files on all assigned personnel.

X. Attend scheduled chaplain assistant staff meetings as directed.

XI. Complete the Orientation Course, Basic Training Course, and Basic Noncommissioned Officer Training during the first membership year.

XII. Attend a minimum of eighty percent of all scheduled monthly meetings to maintain a satisfactory attendance record.

XIII. Prepare and submit all quarterly chaplain assistant reports to the Battalion Chaplain.

XIV. Perform other duties as directed.

✟

Chapter Fourteen:

MILITARY FUNERALS, WEDDINGS, MEMORIALS AND CEREMONIES

Military Funeral Honors for Veterans

For information on military funerals, I recommend checking these sources:

Department of Defense Policy

Strom Thurmond National Defense Authorization Act FY 1999 (Public Law 105-261, Section 567)

Department of Defense Policy, Plans and Procedures (April 21, 1999)

This act and policy puts in place the authority and mandatory directive to the active military to respond properly and on time to comply with requests from families to assist in providing military funerals for veterans. They are to provide a minimum of two military personnel to fold the flag, render and make the flag presentation to the family member, and/or conduct other honors as is appropriate.

Military Funeral Training Outline

I. Introduction: (15 minutes)

Purpose and Functional Procedures

Lesson information: Explain the purpose and historical significance of military funerals, the importance of following protocol in communicating and counseling with the families of the deceased, and coordinating the order of the service with the religious institution and the funeral home director.

II. Training Objectives: (1 hour and 45 minutes)

Proficiency in Conducting the Military Funeral

Lesson information: Proficiency in the conducting of military funerals

A. Task #1: (30 minutes)

Church/Chapel Training

Lesson information:

1. The proper procedures in moving the remains of the deceased from the hearse or caisson into the church/chapel, and from the church/chapel back to the hearse.
2. The order of the procession in and out of the church/chapel.
3. The seating arrangements (coordinated by funeral director).
4. The order of the service (arranged by the chaplain/clergy).

B. Task #2: (30 minutes)

Cemetery Committal Training

Lesson information:

1. The proper procedures in moving the remains of the deceased from the hearse or caisson to the gravesite.
2. The order of the procession/special instructions (funeral director).

3. The seating arrangements (funeral director).
4. The order of the service at the gravesite (chaplain/clergy/NCIOC).

C. Task #3: (30 minutes)
Flag Folding/Presentation
Lesson information:
1. The proper method to fold the flag/firing/taps (chaplain/NCOIC).
2. The presentation of the folded flag to the designated family member (chaplain/NCOIC).
3. The proper words to say to the family as the flag is presented (chaplain/NCOIC).

D. Task #4: (15 minutes)
Practice/Rehearsal—Practice—Practice

Military Funeral Detailed Plans

The military funeral information and study materials have been prepared and written in a format that can be easily understood and followed by an experienced or inexperienced chaplain/minister/pastor to honor the veteran at death. This is the last public opportunity to bestow respect and honor upon a veteran.

The last respect and honor a nation and community can bestow upon an honorably discharged veteran is to conduct a military funeral when such a request has been made by the veteran prior to death, or the request is made by the immediate family at the time of death of their loved one.

Due to the slow reaction on the part of the active military when military funeral requests are made, it has become necessary to establish a backup plan to assist the funeral director and/or the veteran's family when the active military authority does not respond in time for the funeral to be conducted. Future response by the active military to assist in the military funeral should be improved as the result of the attention given to this subject by the senior senator from South Carolina, the Honorable Senator Strom Thurmond (Public Law 105-261, Section 567). We thank Senator Thurmond for his longtime support and fight for veteran's rights.

As an experienced chaplain, I have conducted many military funerals, and as a pastor I am aware of the delays of the active military authorities when a military funeral detail has been requested. Most of the time the active military has a problem organizing personnel in time to meet the funeral schedule, but it is not purposefully planned that way.

It does not take a rocket scientist to see the need for a backup military funeral plan to be in place in the event the active military cannot respond to a request in time. Therefore, two things must be done. First, volunteers (veterans and chaplains) from the community should be recruited to conduct the military funeral. Second, organize, plan and train the volunteers in the proper way to conduct a military funeral.

As a veteran, one does not have to attend many military funerals to see firsthand how appreciative both you and the veteran's family can be to have the military funeral carried out properly. And, on the other hand, it is very embarrassing as a veteran to witness a poorly carried out military funeral . . . the performance of the detail, as well as the manner in which the chaplain assists, must be precise.

There is no acceptable excuse for such a thing to happen. It is outright disregard for the honor and respect being shown to the deceased veteran. It would be easy to say, "If the military funeral cannot be carried out properly, don't do it." It would be better to say, "Let's conduct the military funeral in a proper way. We owe that much to the deceased veteran!"

From this point on, the military funeral instructional materials have been written in layman's language to simplify the procedures. After carefully studying and reviewing the procedures followed by active duty military personnel, I incorporated my own personal knowledge and experience into the revised document. It must be understood that this instructional format is presented as *information* only!

Military funerals, memorial services and memorial ceremonies honor the memory of a deceased veteran. The manner in which the funeral is carried out reflects upon the professionalism of the volunteer chaplain and shows pastoral and spiritual respect for the veteran and family. Volunteer chaplains are to be experienced and qualified clergy, or at least should be, and must possess the skills to convey a sense of understanding and compassion during times of grief. Thus, the chaplain serves an important role in the final tribute to veterans who have served our nation honorably.

The chaplain, when called upon, is to assist the veteran service officer, the funeral director, the cemetery officials, and the family to ensure the propriety and dignity of the final rites of a military funeral. The military funeral basic training will provide the volunteer chaplain with guidance and procedures for conducting military funerals and memorial ceremonies. Its primary focus will be upon rendering support to veterans and their families.[22]

Two Distinct Elements

The military funeral has two distinct elements: military ceremony and religious service. The military ceremony, conducted in a serious and dignified manner, recognizes the service and the sacrifice of the veteran to the nation, and strengthens the spirit of all veterans. Every individual who attends the military funeral should be appropriately reverent, decorous and sensitive to the occasion.

More than that, the military funeral should use the resources of worship so that the Word of God can meet the needs of the mourners. The worship service speaks of faith, joy and assurance, and does not center on eulogizing the life or displaying the body of the deceased. Through religious rite, it also extends spiritual ministry to the veteran's family and the host of friends. It provides a public profession of faith for the religious community and public support for the bereaved. The services in the chapel and at the grave form the worship portions of the military funeral.

The memorial ceremony and the memorial service are also clearly distinct. The memorial service is a religious service. When possible, it is conducted by a chaplain of the distinct faith group of the deceased. Like a funeral service, it is guided by the rites of the chaplain's denomination. The chaplain has broad discretion in the memorial service, which is appropriate for military and nonmilitary personnel.

The memorial ceremony, on the other hand, is patriotic, not denominational. It may be conducted by any chaplain or, in exceptional cases, another appointed layperson. Religious elements are minimal and nondenominational. The memorial ceremony and memorial service may be conducted back to back, separated by a break. When the service is for more than one person, chaplains of respected faiths may jointly conduct the memorial service. For the deceased without religious preference, the memorial ceremony suffices.

Based on the chaplain's advice, a decision is reached whether ceremony or service or both are appropriate. Neither will be held for missing persons (those believed to be deceased, or those known to be deceased but not positively identified).

Roles
The Commander's Staff
The chaplain is the commander's special staff officer in matters pertaining to the religious aspects of military ceremony and memorial services. As such, the chaplain coordinates with the commander and staff for appropriate support.

The Chaplain
The chaplain has a two-fold role when honoring the dead: clergy and staff officer. As clergy, the chaplain is responsible for the religious service. As a military officer, he provides the final tribute to the deceased veteran.

The chaplain serves as pastor, counselor, and friend to the family and friends of the deceased. Pastoral care is given throughout the mourning period. Before and after the funeral service, the chaplain visits and counsels the deceased's loved ones. The chaplain can provide a supportive spirit to the bereaved and help them not only to face the reality of death, but provide them with hope for the future. Religious rites and sacraments are important in the spiritual healing process.

The chaplain's primary role during the military funeral, memorial service and ceremony is to ensure that the proceedings are sensitive to the spiritual and emotional needs of the veteran's family and those attending, and to encourage a positive tone and attitude of those present for an appropriate order of worship.

The Chaplain Assistant (An Enlisted Person)

The chaplain assistant coordinates support for the chaplain throughout the entire process of planning and carrying out the service or ceremony. Under the chaplain's guidance, the chaplain assistant:

- Consults local standing procedures and pertinent regulations.
- Completes necessary administrative tasks.
- Coordinates logistical support and needed supplies.
- Confirms biographical data by consulting the deceased's military personnel records jacket and ensuring the accuracy of the bulletins that are typed.
- Serves as a pallbearer when needed.
- Performs other duties as directed by the chaplain.

The Grief Process

The chaplain will be aware of the grief process when ministering to the family. The first stage of grief is denial and isolation. Feelings may be expressed in such statements as "It can't be so" or "Just leave me alone." The second stage is anger, which may be displaced in all directions, especially towards God. Bargaining is the third stage and feelings of guilt may be expressed. Words such as "If only I would have . . . " are not uncommon. The fourth stage is depression, which can be expressed in a variety of ways, such as feeling tired, lack of interest, weeping and other physical manifestations of sadness. The fifth stage of grief is acceptance.

Throughout the grief process the chaplain will be a compassionate listener and serve as a reminder of God's presence, even in the experience of death. By helping the deceased's loved ones work through their grief, the chaplain can bring them to a place of healing, hope and peace.

Funeral Arrangements
Chaplain Participation

The chaplain will assist in conducting or arranging for the burial of veterans with their immediate family members. When possible, the desires of the family will determine the funeral arrangements. They will decide whether a military funeral will be conducted, which of the authorized honors will be rendered, and where the body will be buried. The family will also decide whether they would like a chaplain or civilian clergyperson to conduct or assist in the service. The chaplain will not be required to perform services that are at variance with the tenets of their religion.

Cultural Differences

The funeral or memorial service must never become routine or impersonal. When possible, the chaplain will respect the wishes and desires of the family and use worship resources that meet the needs of the mourners. Consideration should be given to the native language and cultural differences of a deceased veteran's family.

Because funerals can create much emotional stress, the service itself should be kept short. A well-planned, well-conducted funeral or memorial extends spiritual ministry to those present, and provides public support to the bereaved.

Primary responsibility for completing the funeral arrangements rests with the family. The chaplain will assist the funeral director and cemetery superintendent in carrying out the military funeral.

Funeral Procedures

The funeral service is followed by the move from the chapel to the gravesite or place of local disposition with the prescribed escort.

When the funeral is conducted the chaplain will consult local standard operating procedures for guidance in arranging the funeral.

A military funeral may contain only some of the following elements. However, directions for a full military funeral apply to all military funerals, and include:

- A band
- An escort appropriate to the grade of the deceased, which may include:
  - Firing squad and bugler
  - The colors
  - Hearse or caisson
  - Caparisoned horse (if the deceased was a member of a mounted unit)
  - Active pallbearers
  - Honorary pallbearers

Note: The word "chapel" is interpreted to include the church, synagogue, home, or other place where services are held, other than the gravesite.

Uniforms and Vestments

Because arms will not be borne in the sanctuary of a chapel, church or synagogue, military personnel may wear empty pistol belts. Doing so fulfills the requirements of being under arms while simultaneously showing respect for the sanctuary.

The chaplain in uniform uncovers inside the chapel and covers outside the chapel. All personnel except active pallbearers follow the example of the chaplain in uniform.

Seating Family Members
Before the casket is taken into the chapel, the family, relatives and friends should be asked to enter the chapel. The family may be seated in the right front pews.

Note: The body of the deceased may be taken into the chapel prior to the arrival of family and friends. Friends may enter the chapel upon arrival, and be seated as directed by the funeral director.

Arrival of the Casket
The funeral escort forms a line facing the chapel before the service begins. The hearse or conveyance bearing the deceased should arrive at the chapel a few moments before the time set for the service.

The chaplain will be in position at the curb or chapel door. Since the casket is normally covered by the flag, the escort is called to attention by the escort commander. The escort commander salutes as the conveyance passes.

The chaplain salutes in unison with the escort commander and the OIC/NCOIC (Officer in Charge/Noncommissioned Officer in Charge). If in vestments, the chaplain stands at attention. When all is in readiness to move the casket into the chapel, the funeral director gives the signal to move forward.

Entrance into the Chapel
At the command of the funeral director, the casket is removed from the conveyance by the active pallbearers,

into the chapel. The active pallbearers will be covered and remain covered during the time they escort the remains to the front of the chapel. They will handle the remains in a dignified, reverential and military manner, ensuring that the movement of the casket is feet first at all times and remaining covered during the time they escort the casket to the front of the chapel.

When the casket reaches the chapel door, the chaplain orders arms and leads the procession into the chapel.

When honorary pallbearers are present, they form two ranks, each facing the other, creating an aisle from the conveyance to the entrance of the chapel. At the command of the funeral director, the casket is carried between the ranks of honorary pallbearers, who uncover or salute.

Times to Render the Hand Salute
At the military funeral, military personnel in uniform, in their individual capacity, face the casket and execute the hand salute at the following times:
- When honors are sounded (if provided)
- Whenever the casket is being moved (the exception being when they themselves are moving)
- During cannon salute (if provided)
- During the firing of volleys (if provided)
- While taps is being played (if provided)

Honorary pallbearers in uniform also conform to these instructions, when not in motion.

Military Personnel in Civilian Clothing
Military personnel in civilian clothing in the above cases, and during the service at the gravesite, stand at atten-

tion, and hold their hats over the left side of the chest. If no hat is worn, the right hand is held over the heart.

Positions Inside the Chapel

When the casket has been placed on the church truck, the funeral director and his assistant will push the casket to the front of the chapel while the others wait until they return to the vestibule.

The chaplain, at the direction of the funeral director, precedes the casket and takes his place in front of the altar. If the church truck is used the active pallbearers will, after the chaplain is in position, enter the chapel in pairs.

They will move, under cover, down the aisle slowly, approach the casket and render the hand salute, and then move to the designated seating, but remain standing and covered. The next two active pallbearers will do the same, until all active pallbearers have entered; all active pallbearers will in unison remove their cover, and remain standing until the family of the deceased has been seated.

If there is no church truck, the active pallbearers carry the casket to the front of the chapel and position it as instructed by the funeral director before the service. The active pallbearers will be seated as directed by the funeral director.

Honorary pallbearers will occupy the pews at the front of the chapel, as directed by the funeral director.

Exiting the Chapel

After the service, the funeral director and his assistant will come forward and signal the honorary pallbearers to take their former positions outside the chapel. The honorary pallbearers again form an aisle from the entrance of the chapel to the hearse (or caisson, if provided) and uncover or salute.

The chaplain and the active pallbearers, at the direction of the funeral director, move to the aisle in front of the casket, then proceed to the vestibule of the chapel. The active pallbearers cover once arriving at the vestibule, and line up on either side as the funeral director pushes the church truck, with the casket, to the vestibule.

At the direction of the funeral director, the active pallbearers lift the casket in unison, and the funeral director removes the church truck and takes measures to have the flag in place.

The funeral director directs the chaplain and pallbearers to proceed to the hearse. The chaplain turns and leads the procession out of the chapel. The family group follows the casket.

Outside the chapel, the chaplain resumes his original position at the chapel door or curb, stands at attention, and renders the salute until the casket has been placed in the hearse/conveyance.

Changing Vestments

If the chaplain wants to change from vestments into uniform, the change may be made after the procession to the chapel door. The chaplain may change in the sacristy, as the casket is taken out and placed in the conveyance, and thereafter join the procession.

Forming the Procession

The funeral escort and the band (if provided) repeat the procedure prescribed for entering the chapel. When the casket has been secured in the hearse (or caisson, if provided), the band ceases to play and the escort is brought to the order.

The honorary pallbearers then enter their vehicles. The family group remains at the chapel entrance until the honorary pallbearers have broken ranks to enter their vehicles or taken their positions for marching to the gravesite—if nearby.

As they march, the honorary pallbearers will form columns on each side of the caisson/hearse, with the leading member of each column opposite the front of the conveyance. The family members are then led to their vehicles.

Note: If the chapel is near or on the cemetery grounds, the funeral procession forms in the following manner:
- First: escort commander
- Second: band (if provided)
- Third: escort, including colors, (if provided) firing squad and the bugler (the firing squad and bugler may be positioned at the gravesite)
- Fourth: honorary pallbearers, if riding in vehicles
- Fifth: chaplain/clergy
- Sixth: caisson or hearse, and honorary pallbearers, if walking
- Seventh: active pallbearers
- Eighth: personal flag
- Ninth: caparisoned horse, (if chosen)
- Tenth: family, friends and patriotic or fraternal organizations

When the procession has formed, the escort and the band are put in march by the escort commander. The elements in the rear conform to the orders of the escort commander.

In the event of a vehicle procession, local custom will dictate the order of procession. The family and friends follow the official party (chaplain, pallbearers and the hearse), allowing time for the official party to assume their positions for the graveside service.

If possible, the escort and the band go directly to the cemetery, before the procession leaves the chapel so as to be in place when the procession arrives at the cemetery. This may not be possible in some cases.

Funeral Services Not Conducted at the Chapel

For a funeral which excludes a chapel service, the funeral procession may form at the entrance or at a point within a reasonable distant from the cemetery.

The chaplain may travel with the family to the cemetery. Otherwise, the chaplain must be at the cemetery in advance to meet the family members and the hearse. The chaplain stands next to the OIC/NCOIC at the curb near the graveside and salutes as the hearse passes.

If the chaplain's first personal contact with the family occurs at the cemetery, the chaplain may go to the family car and meet the immediate family, and then return to the original position at the curb. The prescribed procedures for a graveside service are then followed.

Graveside Services

As the procession approaches the grave, the marching (if provided) elements move directly to their predesignated positions. The band and military escort form a line in view of the family.

The other marching elements (if provided) stand as near as practical to the grave. The firing squad (if provided) stands so that it does not fire directly over the mourners, but over the grave and in view of the family.

The chaplain is met at the cemetery by either the cemetery representative or the OIC/NCOIC. They take their positions at the curb and the hearse stops just beyond them. As the flag-draped casket passes, military participants salute.

Arrival of the Caisson/Hearse
As soon as the caisson/hearse stops, the honorary pallbearers form two ranks, creating an aisle which extends from the conveyance toward the grave. The escort commander calls, "Present arms."

The band (if provided) renders honors, if appropriate, followed by a hymn. At the first note of the hymn, the active pallbearers remove the casket from the conveyance.

The chaplain stands to the side rear, facing the conveyance while the remains are transferred. The chaplain and the OIC/NCOIC salute while the casket is removed from the hearse. Ordering arms, the chaplain moves to the head of the casket.

Movement of the Casket to the Gravesite
The chaplain and the funeral director precede the casket as the active pallbearers carry it between the ranks of the honorary pallbearers. As soon as the casket has passed, the honorary pallbearers face the grave and follow the casket in a column of pairs.

They are followed by the family and friends. As the casket is moved from the caisson/hearse to the grave, the escort is brought to present arms. When the casket has been placed over the grave, the band (if provided) ceases to play and the escort is brought to order arms. The commander of the escort then commands, "Parade rest."

At the Graveside

Taking a position near the head of the grave, the chaplain salutes again until the casket is in place. At the graveside, the chaplain in uniform has the option of wearing a head covering.

If the chaplain removes the head covering, all others in uniform, except ceremonial elements, should remove their head covers. When the officiating chaplain wears a yarmulke (Jewish skull cap), all personnel remain covered. The active pallbearers, upon reaching the grave, place the casket on the lowering device. They remain in place facing the casket. They raise the flag from the casket and hold it in a horizontal position, waist-high, until the conclusion of taps.

The Religious Service

The graveside worship is left to the discretion of the officiating chaplain. A simple and brief religious service of Scripture and prayer is appropriate. The religious service may be denominational in character and in keeping with the emotional and spiritual needs of those present. At the conclusion of the religious service, the chaplain moves two steps to the side or rear.

Following the Religious Service

After the benediction at the graveside, three volleys will be fired, followed by the sounding of taps. Immediately after taps have been sounded, the flag will be folded and presented to the chaplain for presentation to the designated family member.

Firing Squad

The firing squad, consisting of not more than eight riflemen and not less than five with a noncommissioned officer in charge, is pre-positioned about 50-75 feet away from the grave itself. They will be facing in a 45-degree angle in the direction that allows them to fire directly over the grave.

After the religious service, the optional "firing party" will be instructed to fire three volleys at the command of the firing party NCOIC. (The chaplain will warn the family beforehand that the three volleys will be fired.)

The firing party fires three volleys and presents arms at the command of the NCOIC. They remain in position until the conclusion of taps. The bugler (if provided), positioned near the firing party and in view of the family, sounds taps immediately after the last volley.

During the playing of taps, the honorary pallbearers and the military personnel in their individual capacity give the appropriate salute. Following taps, the chaplain, if in uniform, assumes staff officer status and renders honors as a representative of the commander in chief.

Folding and Presentation of the Flag

The flag is folded and passed to the OIC/NCOIC at the head of the grave. Whether or not the chaplain presents the flag will be discussed with the OIC/NCOIC prior to the service.

If the chaplain is to present the flag, the OIC/NCOIC faces about and places the flag, at the chest level, into the hands of the chaplain. The active pallbearers face the left and right, respectively, and march away from the grave in a column of twos. The OIC/NCOIC salutes the flag for three seconds and faces about to assume the original position.

The chaplain then presents the flag to the predesignated family member. In doing so, the chaplain may use the expression which has become standard at military funerals: "This flag is presented on behalf of a grateful nation as a token of our appreciation for the honorable and faithful service rendered by your loved one."

The chaplain may then step back one pace and salute. Whether or not the salute is rendered depends upon the personal preference of the chaplain and what is deemed appropriate for the family.

Flag Folding Instructions
Standing north to south, the stars are north, right front end.

1. Fold the lower striped section of the flag over the blue field.
2. Fold again left to right (folded edge to open edge).
3. From the south end, start a triangular fold by bringing the striped corner of the folded edge to the open edge.
4. From the south end fold the outer point inward, parallel with the open edge, to form a second triangle.
5. From the south end, continue the folding until the entire length of the flag is folded into a triangle with only the blue field and margin showing.

Note: The properly-folded flag should resemble a cocked hat.

Variations

Cremation Funeral

For all phases of the funeral, where the receptacle holding the cremated remains is carried by hand, one pallbearer is detailed to carry the receptacle and another to carry the flag, folded into the shape of a cocked hat.

The pallbearer carrying the flag is positioned to the right of the remains. The receptacle is loaded and unloaded before the flag. While the receptacle is carried from the conveyance, and from the chapel back to the conveyance, the two pallbearers are the only participants in the ceremony.

During the procession to the gravesite, the two pallbearers are followed by four additional pallbearers.

The receptacle and the flag are placed side by side before the chancel of the chapel and in the conveyance transporting them to the gravesite. If the two pallbearers are to walk to the gravesite, they will join the four other pallbearers who are pre-positioned on either side of the conveyance.

When no caisson/hearse is used, transportation is provided for the receptacle, flag and the other pallbearers.

When the remains are conducted to a crematory, the ashes are to be interred with military honors at a later time; the ceremony consists only of the escort to the crematory. Arms are presented as the remains are borne into the crematory.

The firing of volleys and the sounding of taps are omitted.

Where the funeral ceremony is held at the crematory and no further honors are anticipated, the volleys (if provided) are fired and taps sounded at the discretion of the OIC/NCOIC.

Note: For dispersion of cremations from an aircraft, private memorials services must be requested and approved.

Joint Funeral Service

When asked to share in a joint worship service, the chaplain is guided by policies set by the denomination or endorsing agent. The chaplain cooperates and is sensitive to the needs of the civilian clergy chosen by the family.

When military dead are buried from a civilian church, synagogue or mortuary, the chaplain may co-officiate at the funeral. In such cases, the chaplain presides when military honors are rendered.

Fraternal or Patriotic Organizations

If the immediate family of the deceased or its representative so requests, organizations of which the deceased was a member may be permitted to take part in the funeral service.

Under no circumstances will the organizations override the chaplain's denominational practices.

Organizations wishing to conduct services at the gravesite may do so, following the playing of taps (if provided), at the conclusion of the military portion of the ceremony. Upon request, the local commander may authorize use of the military firing squad and bugler (if provided) for such services.

Other

It is impossible to anticipate or describe all settings or circumstances in which military funerals may be held. When changes from these guidelines are necessary, those responsible for them should keep in mind the meaning of the worship service and its significance in meeting the emotional and spiritual needs of the mourners.

All variations will exemplify the dignity and honor rendered in a full military funeral.

Rehearsal

Whether it is a military funeral, memorial service or memorial ceremony, the primary participants should meet at least once prior to the event to coordinate the honors and sequence of events outlined by the chaplain or the OIC/NCOIC.

Memorial Service

The memorial service is a religious service. It stresses spiritual comfort to the family, relatives, friends, and especially the deceased's veteran friends. The elements of a memorial service are similar to those of the military funeral.

The chaplain will ensure that the tributes and prayers are appropriate and that they address the spiritual and emotional needs of those who attend. The content can vary depending on the situation and the pastoral decisions of the chaplain. It may involve the posting of colors, prayers, and Scripture reading, music, a tribute to the deceased or addressees and meditations.

In most cases, a worship bulletin, which lists the order of worship and may contain a biographical sketch of the deceased service member, is prepared by the officiating chaplain.

The circumstances should dictate an appropriate order of worship since there is no prescribed order. Basic elements which may be included are:

- Prelude
- Posting of the colors
- National Anthem
- Invocation
- Memorial tribute, biographical sketch, service record
- Scripture reading
- Prayers
- Hymns
- Special music
- Meditation
- Benediction
- Taps

Ceremony

The memorial ceremony is a patriotic tribute to a deceased veteran. The memorial ceremony is a military function, which is normally not conducted in a chapel. Neither religious vestments nor terminology are used.

The content of the memorial ceremony may vary depending on circumstances, the environment, the wishes of the family, and the pastoral advice of the chaplain.

The Basic Elements

The ceremony may be simple, with only a few basic elements, or very involved and formal. Some of the elements which may be included in a memorial ceremony are:

- Prelude
- Posting of the colors (care must be taken to ensure the proper placement of the colors). If the ceremony is held in a chapel, the colors may be posted in their regular places or held by bearers at the front or side of the chapel.
- The ceremony may begin with the presentation and posting of the colors. Pre-positioning them in the chapel would be preferable. Posting of the colors may be omitted in a simple ceremony.
- When a ceremony is held in the field, the colors must be stationed in a prominent position. Colorbearers and guards should wear customary military headgear.
- National anthem: The playing of the national anthem is always appropriate.
- Special music: Music can set the tone for the ceremony. The chapel organist, pianist, choir, or band (if provided) may play or sing a suitable prelude and postlude.
- Memorial tribute, biographical sketch, service record: A reading of the veteran's record.
- Silent tribute: After the memorial tribute, all persons present may stand silently in honor of the deceased veteran. The chaplain is guided in his decisions by good taste, the needs of the family, the spirit of the veteran's friends and the tradition of the service.
- Address or remarks: An appropriate brief address and/or meditation may be given by the chaplain or other veterans/friends. If someone other than the chaplain is to give the address, the chaplain may assist by leading the meditation.
- Volleys
- Taps: The bugler may sound taps from an inconspicuous position.
- Traditions of the military unit served in.

Nondenominational

Since the memorial ceremony is of a patriotic nature, the denominational background of the officiating chaplain makes little difference. Service members of all faiths and denominations will attend the ceremony. Their pluralistic nature must play a major role in planning the ceremony, which should be meaningful without giving offense.

Military Tradition

Whenever they are conducted and whatever their components, military funerals, memorial services and ceremonies belong to a venerable military tradition. Each final tribute draws from the tradition and adds to it, not routinely nor impersonally, but profoundly and compassionately.

Perhaps no group has initiated, and still follows, more funeral/burial traditions than the military, although most of the customs currently in place among the United States armed forces were carried over from the British Army and Navy. The most recognized rituals of a military funeral include draping the casket with the flag, cannon salutes, firing three rifle shots across the gravesite, a 21-gun salute, and the playing of taps. At first, the call now known as taps was reserved to simply signal sundown in military camps and its first use at a funeral was more out of military strategy than anything else. In 1862, according to history, when a deceased soldier was buried, the custom was to fire three shots over the grave, but due to being near enemy troops, a captain decided against firing shots and sounded taps. This way, the enemy would not be alarmed into thinking an attack was coming. A new custom began.

Burial At Sea Ceremonial Procedures

The tradition of burial at sea is an ancient one. As far as anyone knows, this has been a practice as long as people have gone to sea. In earlier times, the body was sewn into a weighted shroud, usually a sailcloth. The body was then sent over the side, usually with an appropriate religious ceremony. Many burials at sea took place during WWII when naval forces operated at sea for weeks and months at a time. Since WWII, many service members, veterans and family members have chosen to be buried at sea.

The burial service may be read by the chaplain of an appropriate religious faith, or if no chaplain is available, the commanding officer or another designated officer. The committal service will be conducted as follows:

- The casket bearers, the firing squad and the bugler will assemble as instructed.
- The officer's call will be sounded, "All hands bury the dead." (The ship should be stopped, if practical to do so, and colors displayed at half-mast.)
- The personnel assemble and stand at attention, adjutant's call.
- The massed formation is called to parade rest.
- Burial Service:
  ❖ The Scripture is read.
  ❖ The prayer is given.
  ❖ The committal (casket or urn under the flag, tilted as committal is sounded, feet first slides into the sea; those present are called to attention, hand salute is given)
  ❖ Benediction
- Firing Squad: three volleys (attention, hand salute)
- Taps
- Encasing of the flag
- Retreat is sounded (resume normal duties)

Burial Requirements for Jewish Military Personnel

- Burial is to take place within 24-48 hours after death (or after discovery of the body).
  - ❖ Another Jewish person should accompany and be with the body at all times until burial.
  - ❖ *Havrah Kadisha* (Holy Society) will wash and prepare the body for burial.
- The body should not be cremated. No bodily fluids should be drained, and any separated body parts should be buried with the body. Autopsies and organ donation are authorized under certain conditions.
- Traditionally, the deceased should not be buried in uniform, but in a simple white *kitel* (gown). Fringes of the *talit* (prayer shawl) should be buried with the deceased. The casket should be made of simple wood with little or no ornamentation.
- The burial ceremony follows both military and Jewish guidelines. A Jewish clergyperson or lay leader will chant several traditional prayers (Kaddish, Al Rachamin, et cetera). Immediate family members may tear the garment as sign of grief. The head covering, or *kippah* (yarmlke), is worn inside the chapel/synagogue and at the gravesite by all in attendance.
- After the burial, immediate family and friends will gather for a simple meal. All mirrors should be covered and the immediate family may sit on the floor.
- The headstone will not be placed until approximately one year after the *yahrzeit* (death).
- The immediate family members start the "sitting shivah" (mourning period) for seven days at this time.

Note: For more information and assistance contact the nearest synagogue or Jewish Chaplains Council in New York at (212) 532-4949.

✟

Chapter Fifteen:

ADDITIONAL INFORMATION

The History of Taps
Version One

The first version of the history of taps is reported to have had its beginning during the Civil War in 1862.

A Union Army soldier, Captain Robert Ellicombe, was commanding his troops near Harrison's Landing in Virginia. The Yankees were on one side of the narrow strip of land, and the Rebels were on the other side.

Sometime during the night Captain Ellicombe heard the loud moan of a soldier who evidently was mortally wounded, and lay dying in the open field. He did not know if the dying man was a Union or Confederate soldier, but Captain Ellicombe decided to risk his life to bring the wounded soldier to his lines for medical treatment.

Captain Ellicombe crawled on his stomach through the gunfire and finally reached the dying soldier. He grabbed the soldier's clothing and began pulling him back toward his side of the landing. When the captain reached his lines safely, he not only discovered that the man was a Confederate soldier, but also that he was dead.

The captain lit a lantern, caught his breath, and went numb with shock. In the dim light of the lantern he saw the face of the soldier . . . it was his own son! The young man had been studying music in the South when the war broke out and without telling his father, he had enlisted in the Confederate Army.

The following morning the heartbroken father asked permission of his commander to give his son a full military burial, despite the young man's enemy status. The captain's request was partially granted.

The father asked if he could have a group of Army band members play a tune during the burial of his son.

His request was refused, since the soldier was a Confederate. However, out of respect for the captain, the commander said he could loan him one musician. The captain chose a bugler. The bugler was asked by the father to play a series of musical notes found in the pocket of his dead Confederate son's uniform. This wish was granted. The music notes previously written by the dead son were the musical notes played by the bugler. The music was the haunting bugle melody we now know as taps.

Version Two

The most inspiring "bugle call" of the military, taps, is believed to have been created during the Civil War by a 30-year-old Union Congressional Medal of Honor recipient, Major General Daniel Butterfield.

He had been seriously wounded in battle while performing many acts of bravery under fire. As he lay among the wounded, dead, and bloody soldiers, he began to comfort their spirits as best he could by whistling a made-up tune.

It has been reported by many people down through the years that one week after the June 1862 Battle of Gaines Mill, near Richmond, Virginia, General Butterfield could not get what he had seen out of his mind. He felt the living needed some type of tune, something to comfort them and remind them of the great loss of the soldier.

On the night of July 1, 1862, he began turning various musical phrases over in his mind, searching for just the right combination of notes that would boost the morale of his men.

The next morning, he sent for his brigade bugler, Oliver Norton, and whistled the simple, yet touching tune he had settled on. The bugler blew the 24-note melody several times as the general hummed and whistled changes until he was satisfied with the call. Norton wrote down the notes on an old piece of paper. He studied it and practiced the melody until he had it down pat. Later that evening, at the request of General Butterfield he played taps for the troops.

The music was beautiful on that still summer night, and was heard beyond the limits of the brigade as it echoed through the trees, hills and valleys.

The next morning, buglers from other brigades came to inquire about the new taps and to learn how to sound it. Only days later the tradition of playing taps at military funerals had its beginning. Also incorporated into the funeral ceremony was the rifle firing salute of three volleys.

An Army captain, fearing the traditional firing of rifle volleys over a soldier's grave might trigger shooting from the Confederate lines, instructed his bugler to just sound taps. The call quickly spread throughout the Army. It was even picked up by the Confederates, who played it at the funeral of General Stonewall Jackson in 1863.

Taps was officially adopted by the Army in 1874, and has been used for lights out, military funerals and memorial services ever since.

General Butterfield died in 1901 and was buried at the U.S. Military Academy at West Point. Taps was sounded. The sound of the mournful, yet thrilling tune he had given to his country, will forever be an honor to his memory.

Our United States American Flag

On August 3, 1949, President Harry Truman signed a law designating June 14 as National Flag Day, honoring the anniversary of the Flag Resolution of 1777.

The rules and customs of how the flag will be displayed and flown are in accordance with the July 7, 1976 amendment to the Flag Code (Public Law 94-344, 94th Congress, S. J. res. 49).

Who Made the Flag?

Betsy Ross has become one of the most cherished figures in American history. On June 14, 1777, the Continental Congress, in order to establish an official flag for the new nation, passed the first Flag Act. It mandated that the flag of the United States "be made of thirteen stripes, alternate red and white; that the union be thirteen stars, white in a blue field, representing a new constellation."

The Continental Congress left no record to show why it chose the colors. However, in 1982, the Congress of the Confederation chose these same colors for the Seal of the United States and listed their meanings as follows:
- White to mean purity and innocence.
- Red for valor and hardness.
- Blue for vigilance, perseverance, and justice.

Betsy Ross sewed the flag, but it is believed the designer was Francis Hopkinson, a New Jersey delegate to the Continental Congress and a signer of the Declaration of Independence. No one knows what happened to the first flag. Very few flags from that time have survived.

Calling the flag "Old Glory" came about in 1831 when Captain William Driver, a shipmaster from Salem, Massachusetts, left on one of his many voyages. Friends presented him with a flag of twenty-four stars. As the banner opened to the ocean breeze, Captain Driver remarked, "Old Glory." He kept his flag for many years, protecting it during the Civil War, until it was flown over the Tennessee capital. His "Old Glory" became a nickname for all American flags.

Flag Holidays
New Year's Day — January 1
Inauguration Day — January 20
Lincoln's Birthday — February 12
Washington's Birthday — Third Monday in February
Easter Sunday — Variable
Mother's Day — Second Sunday in May
Armed Forces Day — Third Saturday in May
Memorial Day — Last Monday in May (Half-staff until noon)
Flag Day — June 14
Independent Day — July 4
Labor Day — First Monday in September
Constitution Day — September 17
Columbus Day — Second Monday in October
Navy Day — October 27
Veterans Day — November 11
Thanksgiving Day — Fourth Thursday in November
Christmas Day — December 25

The birthdays of states (date of admission) and state holidays may be considered flag holidays, as well as other days proclaimed by the president of the United States.

The National Flag

The national flag represents our living country and is considered to be a living emblem of the respect and pride we have for our nation. Our flag is a precious possession. Display it proudly!

There are certain fundamental rules of heraldry which, if understood, generally indicate the proper method of displaying the flag:

- The right arm, which is the sword arm and the point of danger, is the place of honor.
- The union of the flag is the place of honor or the honor point.

The national emblem is a symbol of our great country, our heritage and our place in the world. We owe reverence and respect to our flag. It represents the highest ideals of individual liberty, justice and equal opportunity for all.

Pledge of Allegiance

I pledge allegiance to the flag of the United States of America and to the republic for which it stands, one Nation under God, indivisible, with liberty and justice for all.

General Display

- It is the general custom to display the flag in the open from sunrise to sunset on buildings and on stationary flagstaffs. When a patriotic effect is desired, the flag may be flown twenty-four hours a day, if properly illuminated during the hours of darkness.

- The flag should be hoisted briskly and ceremoniously.

- The flag should not be displayed on days when the weather is inclement, except when an all-weather flag is displayed.

- The flag should be displayed daily, on or near the main administration building of every public institution, in or near every polling place on election days, during school days in or near the every schoolhouse.

- No other flag or pennant should be placed above, or if on the same level, to the right of the flag of the United States of America, except during church services conducted by at-sea chaplains for personnel of the military, when the church pennant may be flown above the flag.

- No person shall display the flag of the United Nations or any other national or international flag in a position of equal or superior prominence or honor to, or in place of, the flag of the United States at any place within the United States or any territory or possession thereof. However, there is a provision which states that nothing in the law shall make unlawful the continuance of the practice followed of displaying the flag of the United Nations in a position of superior prominence or honor with that of the U.S. flag at U.N. headquarters in the United States.

- The flag of the United States, when it is displayed with another flag against a wall from crossed staffs, should be on the right, the flag's own right, and its staff should be in front of the staff of the other flag.

- The flag of the United States should be at the center and at the highest point of the group when a number of flags of states or localities or pennants of societies are grouped and displayed from staff.

- When flags of states, cities, or localities, or pennants of societies, are flown on the same halyard with the flag of the United States, the latter should always be at the peak. When the flags are flown from adjacent staffs, the flag of the United States should be hoisted first, and lowered. No such flag or pennant may be placed above the flag of the United States or to the United States flag's right.

- When the flags of two or more nations are displayed, they are to be flown from separate staffs of the same height. The flags should be of approximately equal size. International usage forbids the display of the flag of one nation above that of another nation in time of peace.

- When the flag of the United States is displayed from a staff projecting horizontally or at a right angle from the window sill, balcony, or front of a building, the union of the flag should be placed at the peak of the staff unless the flag is at half-staff. When the flag is suspended over a sidewalk from a rope extending from a house to a pole at the edge of the sidewalk, the flag should be hoisted out, union first, from the building.

- When displayed either horizontally or vertically against a wall, the union should be uppermost and to the flag's own right, that is, to the observer's left. When displayed in a window, the flag should be displayed in the same way, with the union or blue field tothe left of the observer in the street.

- When the flag is displayed over the middle of the street, it should be suspended vertically with the union to the north in a street running east and west, or to the east in a street running north and south.

- The flag should *never:*
  - ❖ be displayed with the union down, except as a signal of dire distress in instances of extreme danger to life or property.
  - ❖ touch anything beneath it, such as the ground, the floor, water, or merchandise.
  - ❖ be fastened, displayed, used, or stored in such a manner as to permit it to be easily torn, soiled, or damaged in any way.
  - ❖ be used as a covering for a ceiling.
  - ❖ have placed upon it, nor on any part of it, nor attached to it any mark, insignia, letter, word, figure, design, picture, or drawing of any nature.
  - ❖ be used as a receptacle for receiving, holding, carrying, or delivering anything.

Parades and Ceremonies

The flag, when carried in a procession, or with another flag or flags, should be either on the marching right (the flag's own right), or, if there is a line of other flags, in front of the center of that line.

The flag *should:*

- not be displayed on a float in a parade except from a staff (or as against a wall or in a window).
- form a distinctive feature of the ceremony of unveiling a statue or monument. But, it should never be used as the covering for the statue or monument.
- be shown to be the flag of the United States; the flag should not be dipped to any person or thing. Regimental colors, state flags, and organizational flags are to be dipped as a mark of honor.
- never be carried flat or horizontally, but always aloft and free.

During the ceremony of hoisting or lowering the flag when the flag is passing in a parade or in review, all persons present except those in uniform, should face the flag and stand at attention with the right hand over the heart. Those present in uniform should render the military salute. When not in uniform, men should remove their headdress with their right hand and hold it at the left shoulder, the hand being over the heart. Aliens should stand at attention. The salute to the flag in a moving column should be rendered at the moment the flag passes.

Folding the Flag

To fold the flag ceremoniously, first fold it lengthwise, bringing the striped half over the blue field. Then repeat, with the blue field on the outside. Beginning at the lower right, make a series of triangular folds until the flag resembles a cocked hat with only the blue field visible.

Vehicles

The flag should not be draped over the hood, top, sides, or the back of a vehicle or a railroad train or boat. When the flag is displayed on a motor vehicle, the staff shall be fixed firmly to the chassis or clamped to the right fender.

Corridors and Lobbies

When the flag is suspended across a corridor or lobby in a building with only one main entrance, it should be suspended vertically with the union of the flag to the observer's left upon entering. If the building has more than one main entrance, the flag should suspended vertically near the center of the corridor or lobby with the union to the north when entrances are to the east, or west, or to the east when entrances are to the north or south. If there are entrances in more than two directions, the union should be to the east.

Churches and Auditoriums

When used on a speaker's platform, the flag, if displayed flat, should be displayed above and behind the speaker. When displayed from a staff in a church or public auditorium, the flag of the United States should hold the position of superior prominence, in advance of the audience, and in the position of honor at the clergy's or speaker's right as he faces the audience. Any other flag so displayed should be placed on the left of the clergy or speaker, right of the audience.

Caskets

When the flag is used to cover a casket, it should be placed so that the union is at the head and over the left shoulder. The flag should not be lowered into the grave or allowed to touch the ground.

National Anthem

During the rendition of the national anthem when the flag is displayed, all present except those in uniform should stand at attention facing the flag with the right hand over the heart. Those present not in uniform should remove their headdress with their right hand and hold it at the left shoulder, the hand being over the heart. Persons in uniform should render the military hand salute at the first note of the anthem and retain this position until the last note. When the flag is not displayed, those present should face toward the music and act in the same manner they would if the flag were displayed there.

Pledge of Allegiance

The Pledge of Allegiance to the flag should be rendered by standing at attention facing the flag with the right hand over the heart. When not in uniform, those present should remove their headdress with the right hand and hold it at the left shoulder, the hand being over the heart. Persons in uniform should remain silent, face the flag, and render the military salute.

Half-Staff

The flag, when flown at half-staff, should be first hoisted to the peak for an instant and then lowered to the half-staff position. The flag should be again raised to the peak before it is lowered for the day. On Memorial Day, the flag should be displayed at half-staff until noon only, then raised to the top of the staff. On the following days, the flag is to be flown at half-staff for the entire day: December 7—Pearl Harbor Day; May 15—Peace Officers' Memorial Day; July 27—Korean War Veterans' Armistice Day.

By order of the president, the flag shall be flown at half-staff upon the death of principal figures of the United States government and the governor of a state, territory or possession, as a mark of respect to their memory. In the event of the death of other U.S. officials or foreign dignitaries, the flag is to be displayed at half-staff according to presidential instructions or orders, or in accordance with recognized customs or practices not inconsistent with the law.

In the event of the death of a present or former official of the government of any state, territory or possession of the United States, the governor of that state, territory or possession may proclaim that the national flag may be flown at half-staff.

Wearing Apparel and Drapery

The flag should never be used as a wearing apparel, bedding, or drapery. It should never be festooned, drawn back or up in folds, but always allowed to fall free. Bunting of blue, white, and red, always arranged with the blue above, the white in the middle, and the red below, should be used for covering a speaker's desk, draping the front of a platform, and for decorating in general.

No part of the flag should ever be used as a costume or athletic uniform. However, a flag patch may be affixed to the uniform of military personnel, firemen, policemen, and members of patriotic organizations. The flag represents a living country and is itself considered a living thing. Therefore, the lapel flag pin, being a replica, should be worn on the left lapel near the heart.

Advertising

The flag should never be used for advertising purposes in any manner whatsoever. It should not be embroidered on such articles as cushions or handkerchiefs and the like, printed or otherwise impressed on paper napkins or boxes or anything that is designed for temporary use and discard. Advertising signs should not be fastened to a staff or halyard from which the flag is flown.

Disposal

The flag, when it is in such condition that it is no longer a fitting emblem for display, should be destroyed in a dignified way, preferably by burning.

Military Weddings

Military weddings are not all that different from civilian weddings. The main differences are the groom, or the bride, and the wedding party will be in uniform. A saber arch is usually formed for the couple to depart the church or chapel. Also, a saber is used to cut the cake, rather than a knife. Sometimes the groom's military friends will arrange special transportation to the reception, such as a horse-drawn caisson, for the couple. Frequently the national and unit colors are crossed behind the position of the chaplain. Military weddings often take place on post with the reception at the Officer's Club, but the wedding can take place anywhere. Uniforms are what really make a military wedding.

The formality of the wedding is determined by the bride and the groom and the uniforms they choose. The trend is to dress more formally the later the wedding occurs in the day. A morning wedding is usually less formal than the evening one.

A saber arch is not necessary, but it adds a nice touch. It offers a beautiful choice for pictures, too. Usually there are six to eight uniformed persons to form the saber arch. However, if military persons are not to be a part of the saber arch, the bride and groom may have other special individuals to make the saber arch. Only the bride and the groom will pass under the saber arch.

It is the chaplain's responsibility to insure that all of the state laws are followed when conducting a wedding ceremony, as well as those of the individual's religious faith. A premarital instruction or counseling, rehearsal, and other necessary sessions will be conducted by the chaplain prior to the wedding date/time.

Both military and civilian weddings must be coordinated and authorized before being conducted at a military chapel or church. This is not the responsibility of the chaplain.

Military Staff Study

The following is a recommended standard military staff study. A few tips to follow are:

- Stay strictly within the guidelines of each section.
- Keep each paragraph clear and concise.
- Stay focused and don't insert material or information not required.
- Stick to the approved format.
- The grammar, spelling and punctuation must be perfect.

Military Staff Study Sample

Subject: _____ (Sufficient for file identification)

1. Problem

The first paragraph is a concise statement of the problem in the form of a mission stated in the infinitive area (for example, to determine). If the problem is complex, show the scope. Sub-paragraphing may be used.

2. Assumption

Paragraph two lists any assumptions necessary for a logical discussion of the problem. Assumptions are used in the absence of factual data to constitute a basis for the study and broaden or limit the problem. The assumption, while not a fact, must have a basis in fact. Assumptions are always written in future or conditional tenses.

3. Facts Bearing on the Problem

Paragraph three contains statements of undeniable facts having influence on the problem or its solution. Care is exercised to exclude unnecessary facts because they confuse the issue. Some facts may be uncovered during the research, while others are inherent in the directive assigning the problem. Facts should be listed in a sequence which permits logical development in the discussion paragraph. A reference should be provided for facts which are not a matter of common knowledge.

4. Discussion

Paragraph four includes the detailed analysis of all relevant factors, including the advantages and the disadvantages of possible solutions to the problem. In this paragraph, the action officer sets down, in a clear and concise manner, an objective of the data secured during the research. In a lengthy or complicated staff study, this paragraph may be only a summary, with details included in a discussion annex. Care must be exercised in setting down the discussion to ensure that each item is placed in proper perspective.

5. Conclusion

Paragraph five presents the conclusions drawn from the analysis of all relevant factors, all possible solutions to the problem, and all factors that affect these solutions. Conclusions must follow logically from the previous paragraphs. No new material should be introduced in the conclusions. At least one conclusion must directly answer the problem statement.

6. Recommendations

Paragraph six contains one or more statements addressing what should be done to implement the conclusions. Recommendations must be in agreement with the conclusions. The staff action must be complete. If it is recommended, for example, that a letter should be signed by the commander, the actual letter should be attached to the study as the first annex.

Name
Rank, Branch
Position Title

Annexes (list all attachments)
Concurrences/Nonconcurrences
(Officer Title, i.e., G3, G1, or Chief of Staff, etc.)

Concur _____Nonconcur _____

Each staff officer (section head) shows concurrence/nonconcurrence by signing their name, followed by their rank. The reasons for nonconcurrence should be briefly stated here or on a separate page that will become an additional annex to the staff study.

Annexes Added:

List the annexes, if any, containing nonconcurrences and considerations of nonconcurrences.

Action by Approving Authority

Approved (disapproved), including (excluding) exceptions.

_____
Signature of Commanding Officer

Military Dining-out Guidelines

The dining-out has become a military tradition, and is believed to have originated with the British in establishing traditions of mess rules, out of which arose the formal dining-in. Some of the British customs were clearly intended to have a restraining influence upon the conduct of young junior officers. It has been said they were integrated as part of the "grooming" process for positions of responsibility in later years.

In Britain, the formal dining-in is a required function for officers of a given unit. While the dinner function follows prescribed rules, the latter part of the evening is designed to further comradeship and esprit de corps. One of the prime rules of the dining-in is that no matter what occurs, no word of it is to be spoken outside of the dining-in.

The dining-in became an integral part of the military tradition of all branches of the armed forces of the United States after WWII. It provides an occasion for officers to meet socially at a formal military function as well as an excellent way to say "farewell" and "hello." It also provides a vehicle to recognize individual and unit achievement. Traditionally, it is a formal evening for officers designed to build and maintain esprit de corps. The military further refined the tradition to include the dining out. This function opens the mess dinner to non-unit members, and allows them to be drawn into the inner circle of the group.

Dining-out Format
Instructions
Election of the Mess President and Mr. Vice
A dining-out committee will be established. The committee will elect the Mess President, Mr. Vice of the mess and plan the dining-out date, time, place, and the establishment of an invitation roster.

Function and Participants:
Mr. Vice calls the members to dinner. All participants should proceed to the dinner hall and remain standing behind their chairs.
Mr. Vice announces, "The smoking lamp is out." (No smoking and no cocktails in the dining area.)
The Mess President formally calls the mess to order with one rap of the gavel and the announcement is made, "The mess is opened."
Invocation (Conducted by the chaplain, with all members standing.)

Toasts (All members remain standing.)

President of the Mess: "To our Commander in Chief, the President of the United States."

Members respond together, "To the President."

Mr. Vice toasts, "To . . ."

Members respond, "To . . ."

President of the Mess toasts, "To . . ."

Members respond, "To . . ."

More Toasts (Membership makes toasts in same manner.)

President of the Mess seats the mess, makes welcoming remarks and introduces the head table guests and honored guests.

President of the Mess: "Mr. Vice?"

Mr. Vice: "Yes, Mr. President."

President of the Mess: "A toast to our distinguished guests."

Members rise and guest are announced.

Mr. Vice: "To our honored guests."

Members respond, "Hear, hear."

President of the Mess: "The mess be seated." (Directs members to be seated and begin eating.)

Mr. Vice: "Ladies and gentlemen, this meal is fit for human consumption." (The mess begins to eat main course, desert and coffee/tea or water.)

Note: Mr. Vice controls the program. All members remain seated and continue eating unless called upon by Mr. Vice. Remember, no smoking in the dining area while the lamp is out!

President of the Mess: "The mess is adjourned for fifteen minutes."

Mr. Vice: "The smoking lamp is lit."

Members are allowed to smoke in designated areas.

President of the Mess reopens the mess with one rap of the gavel.

Mr. Vice: "The smoking lamp is out."

President of the Mess makes remarks and introduces the guest speaker.

Guest Speaker speaks.
President of the Mess thanks the guest speaker, and proposes a toast, "Mr. Vice, I propose a toast."
Mr. Vice: "Yes, Mr. President."
President of the Mess: "A toast to our distinguished speaker."
Members and guests: "Hear, Hear."
Note: Additional toasts may be proposed by the President of the Mess.
President of the Mess makes closing remarks.
Benediction is conducted by the chaplains.
All members and guests stand.
President of the Mess adjourns the mess with two raps of the gavel.

Tribute to Veterans Annual Banquet Sample
The last honor, respect and tribute the public can pay to a veteran, without a doubt, is for the family to show that honor by having a military funeral for the deserving deceased veteran. The public can show their respect, honor and tribute by attending a veteran's funeral. However, veterans that are still alive must be honored, respected and a tribute extended annually. We recommend the following tribute to pay that respect and honor.

Annual Veterans' Tribute Banquet Instructions
Let's not fool ourselves, it will take time, funding and volunteers to plan and conduct the annual banquet. The event to be conducted will consist of a minimum of six elements; they are:
  • Staff of volunteers
  • Time for planning and implementing the event
  • Funding
  • Veterans as guests
  • Date/time/place
  • Food

Staff

The first thing to do is to organize an Annual Veterans' Tribute Banquet Committee consisting of five to nine members. Elect a chairperson, vice chairperson, secretary and treasurer. The chairperson will guide the committee in planning and conducting the event and coordinating the program.

Funding

The event should be conducted without the veteran and wife (guest) having to pay a banquet registration fee.

Suggestions

- Arrive at a maximum seating capacity for veterans and guests.
- Divide the total event expenditure cost by the number of seats to arrive at a cost per seat.
- Seek sponsorship of one hundred dollars from a business, a church and/or individuals for the number of seats this will support. Invite the sponsor and his/her guest to attend and extend an invitation to a veteran and his/her guest or to a widow of a veteran (if the sponsor cannot attend, the invitation to two veterans and their guests or widows can be substituted).
- Coordinate the menu with your food service contractor.
- Program planning:
  - Guest speaker
  - Color guard
  - Door prizes
  - Dress
  - P.A. system
  - Program outline/handout
  - Special awards/recognition/remembrance (POWs, Medal of Honor recipients, MIAs, et cetera.)
  - Advertisement

Chaplain Confidential Personnel Information Form

Sample Form

Name _____ Rank _____ Position _____

Address _____City _____ St ___ ZIP ___

ID#_____DOB_____Unit Assigned _____

In case of an emergency or death, please notify: Tel ___

Wife/Next of Kin _____Relationship _____

Address _____City _____St ___ ZIP_____

In case of death, I request the following services and ceremonies be provided me, if possible. (My religious faith group is _____.)

Instructions are:

_____

_____

_____

_____

Funeral Home _____ Burial Place _____

Address_____

_____

S/ _____ Date _____ TEL _____

Recorded by Chaplain _____Rank ____ Position ____

CC: 201 File

Chaplain Confidential Personnel File

Chaplain Chapel/Worship Service
Attendance and Funds Received

Date _____

Chaplain _____Rank _____ Position _____

Chaplain Assistant _____ Rank _____ Position _____

Guests _____Rank _____ Position _____

_____

_____

First Chapel Service: Location _____ Time _____

Attendance _____

Offerings Received _____

Message by _____

Comments _____

_____

Second Chapel Service: Location _____ Time _____

Attendance _____

Offerings Received _____

Message by _____

Comments _____

_____

Consolidate Funds Received _____

Witness: S/_____ Date _____

Witness: S/_____ Date _____

Chaplain: S/ _____ Date _____

CC: Supervisory Chaplain

Chapel/Worship Service File

Letters of Condolence/Concern (Sample)

July 22, 1999

Mrs. William P. Doe
3305 Revelon Drive
Southland, MD 21666

Dear Mrs. Doe:

The medical and chaplain staff at Veteran's Memorial Hospital joins with me in extending to you our deepest sympathy on the death of your son, PFC Edward M. Doe.

We know the irreparable loss that you have suffered and fully realize there is little that we can say to help you in this moment of sorrow. We hope you will find some comfort in knowing that everything was done for him during his last illness. Also, I would like to inform you that his thoughts were of you. He confided in me by expressing his belief and faith in God. He stated that you had instilled in him a love for Christ, and all throughout his childhood, even until now, he remembered. His love for you and your family added strength to his life, and gave him a mysterious power that he used to fight a little longer.

In time, you may find personal reassurance in the thought that he died in the service of his country, and that our gratitude as a nation is deep and lasting.

Our heartfelt condolences are extended to you and the members of your family in your bereavement.

Sincerely yours,

Marshall Parks,
Chaplain, COL, U.S.A

Letter of Concern (Sample)

July 29, 2000

Mr. and Mrs. Thomas Doubters
305 Royal Drive
South Point, NC 28667

Dear Mr. and Mrs. Doubters:

The recent vehicle accident which resulted in the hospitalization of your son, Charles, was unfortunate. We are deeply concerned and extend our sincere wishes for his rapid full recovery. He remains in our daily thoughts and meditations, and we look forward to his return to duty.

I recently visited with Charles, and in discussing his condition with the attending doctor, he has revealed the extent of his injuries to be a strained back, minor internal bleeding, and a broken leg, and his prognosis is good. Please be advised that he continues to receive the best possible medical care available. You will continue to be advised of his recovery. If I can be of further assistance, please do not hesitate in contacting me.

Our thoughts will continue to be with you during this period of uncertainty.

Sincerely yours,

Edward Post
Chaplain, LCDR, U.S.N

Sample Prayers

God, our Father, for the privilege of prayer when we creatures of time and space may have communication and fellowship with the Creator who resides in eternity and time, we praise thy Holy Name.

Hear, O Lord, the prayers of praise, confession, intercession, and petition that are offered up this day from believers in every realm.

Grant thy continuing benediction and blessing with consoling gifts of the Holy Spirit upon those servants and their immediate family members as they make adjustments here to the passing into life eternal of their loved ones.

We pray for our earth that you created so beautiful and good. You willed that man should live in a garden. Grant, O Lord, that the world may yet be saved through your grace and your plan of redemption. In the name of the Son of God, Jesus Christ.

Amen

God, our Father, we never cease to marvel at the provisions that you make to meet the physical and spiritual needs of your creatures.

Your highest creatures, the human race, need only to use aright the gifts you have given us.

We stand in awe of your power that keeps the planets and the stars suspended, and speeding through the tracks of space. Yet, how wonderful it is to know that you are sensitive to the fall of every bird, and the faint whispers of the hopes and needs of the human spirit.

Some of these we speak of in our prayers.

Even as we pray for wisdom to make good choices today, we sing the praises of Him who is the light of this world. We are startled to hear that He said to us of faith, "You are the Light of the World."

Amen

Prayers for Terminal Patients
Protestant

Heavenly Father, I do fully confess unto you all my sins. I promise to serve you and love you with my whole heart. I give my life to you and pray that you will forgive all my sins by which I have offended you on the merits of Christ's death on the cross for me. I receive again that life given to me by His glorious resurrection from the dead. Give me eternal salvation because I believe in you and your promises. I know that God so loved the world that He gave His only begotten Son, and that whosoever believes in Him should not perish but have everlasting life. I offer my prayer in Jesus Christ's name, and I believe.

Amen

Catholic

My God, I am really and truly sorry that I have sinned against you, and I turn away from these sins because I want to go to heaven. The thought of hell makes me terrified. My sins hurt you, my God, and they are against you only. You are truly good to me and deserve only my love and perfect trust. With your good help and grace, enable me to confess my sins, to repent and to change my life. Through Christ our Lord.

Amen

Jewish

Father of mercies, my life and my death are in thy Hands. Thou art one, eternal and all-powerful. Heal me, and I shall be healed.

But if in thy wisdom thou has differently decreed concerning me, I will humbly submit to thy will, praying that all my pain and my suffering at this time is acceptable in thy sight, O Lord, my strength and my redeemer and an atonement for all my errors. "Hear, O Israel: The Lord our God is one Lord."

Shalom

Notes on Prayer

- In the absence of a Jewish chaplain, a non-Jewish chaplain could comfort and offer spiritual assistance to Jewish persons by using the following references. Avoid using references to the New Testament or Christological readings and prayers. (Psalms 23, 70, 103:1-5)
- When ministering to a Catholic by a Protestant or Jewish chaplain, care should be taken to provide for the religious requirements of the individual. One should not violate his conscience/beliefs. The chaplain should be careful to minister fully as he/she would in any other case. The intention of the chaplain ministering should be to offer a simple, direct prayer in compassionate and personal terms seeking the comfort and consolation of God and asking His forgiveness and assistance in handling pain and suffering.
- Ministering to a Protestant by a Catholic or Jewish chaplain should not violate the religious practice and conscience of the individual. The goal is to leave the person with encouragement, comfort and hope by offering a prayer which should be led by the chaplain. If possible, the Lord's Prayer should be recited in unison with the closing: "For Thine is the Kingdom, and the Power, and the Glory, forever and ever. Amen."
- If the individual's religious faith is Lutheran, Episcopal, United Methodist, Presbyterian,or another faith which permits the free use of the recitation of the Apostle's Creed, follow this order.

Call to Worship Recommendations

The Lord is coming, and now is, when the true worshippers will worship the Father in Spirit and in Truth, for such the Father seeks to worship Him.

Invocation

Almighty God, you have given us grace at this time with one accord to make our common supplications unto you, and have promised that you will hear the prayer of faith. Fulfill now, O Lord, the desires and petitions of your servants, granting us in this world knowledge of your truth, and in the world to come, life everlasting.

Amen

Prayer of Confession

We confess to God Almighty, the Father, the Son and the Holy Ghost, and before the whole company of the faithful, that we have sinned exceedingly in thought, word, and deed, through our own fault; wherefore we pray for God to have mercy upon us. Almighty God, have mercy upon us, forgiving us our sins and delivering us from evil, confirming and strengthening us in all goodness, and bringing us to everlasting life.

Amen

Assurance of Pardon

If we confess our sins to God, we can trust Him, for He does what is right. He will forgive us our sins and make us clean from all our wrongdoings.

The Lord's Prayer

Our father, who art in Heaven, hallowed be thy Name, thy kingdom come, thy will be done, on earth as it is in Heaven. Give us this day our daily bread, and forgive us our trespasses, as we forgive those who trespass against us. And, lead us not into temptation, but deliver us from evil. For thine is the kingdom, and the power, and thy glory, forever and ever.

Amen

Pastoral Prayer

Almighty God, who knows our hearts, desires, and secrets; cleanse our thoughts and hearts in the presence of your Holy Spirit, that we may perfectly love you and glorify your name through Jesus our Lord.

Amen

Benediction

We commit you unto God. May He look upon you with His grace, and give you all spiritual blessings, that in this life, and in the life to come, you may be partakers of His grace for all eternity. Go now in love, as those called to do His work. And may God's peace, favor, and mercy bless you always.

Amen

Recommended Order of Services

    Sample #1

    Prelude

    Doxology

    Hymn #_____

    First Reading

    Responsive Reading   *Psalms 139: 1-11, 23-24*

    Second Reading

    Message for the Day   *Chaplain* _____

    Special Music

    Prayer of the Faithful

    The congregation is invited to pray aloud at the appointed time or pray silently during this time.

    Lord's Prayer   *All Pray Together*

    Benediction

    Closing Hymn #_____

    Dismissal: *Chaplain*: "Go in peace. Serve the Lord."
             Congregation: "Thanks be to God."

Sample #2
The Gathering
Invocation
Hymn
Responsive Reading (Old Testament)
The Lord's Prayer
Special Music
Morning Message
Benediction

Sample #3
Welcome
Call to Worship

Responsive Reading:
 Chaplain: Unto thee, O Lord, I lift up my soul
 All: O my soul, I trust in thee; Let me not be
  ashamed
 Chaplain: Yea, let none that wait on thee be ashamed
 All: Show me thy paths, O Lord.Teach me thy ways
 Chaplain: For thou art the God of my salvation
 All: On thee I do wait all the day
 Chaplain: Let integrity and uprightness preserve me
 All: For I wait on thee.

Hymn
Prayer of Confession
Old Testament Reading
New Testament Reading
Message
Benediction

Sample #4

Call to Worship:

Chaplain: We have come to this place, some from far away, some from nearby, some with troubled hearts and minds. May God's spirit unite us in love as we join our hearts and minds to worship God.

People: To affirm with praise and thanksgiving the goodness of the Lord.

Chaplain: Let us rejoice in His presence with us in worship. Let us acknowledge His continuing goodness toward us and our nation.

People: Our lips can shout for joy, for His love covers all that He has made. Blessed be the name of Jesus forever.

Congregational Prayer of Confession:

O God, our Father, from whom we come and unto whom our spirits return, we confess that we are sinners. We asking forgiveness. We confess our reluctance to submit our wills to your will. Restore our faith today. Help us to trust in your Fatherly goodness at all times. In Jesus' name we pray. Amen

Words of Assurance

Responsive Reading:

Chaplain: How great and glorious is our God. From hour to hour, our lives ought to overflow with praise and gratitude.

People: It is amazing, how our God touches every facet of our lives and works out His purposes despite our human failures.

Chaplain: He creates beauty out of the dust of our fallen nature. Out of the ashes of our failures, He brings forth meaning and purpose.

People: He exalts the humble and enriches the poor. He transforms our weaknesses into channels of strength.

Chaplain: Our emptiness becomes a vessel of His fullness, our spiritual poverty the basis for His eternal grace.

People: Our mistakes become stepping stones to success. Our defeats are learning experiences on the road to victory.

Chaplain: But this is God's doings, not ours. How great and glorious is our God!

Message
Scripture: _____
The Ministry of the Lord's Supper

Parting Words:

People: We have given thanks to Him from whom comes life and death. We have affirmed our faith and rejoiced in the knowledge that we will have victory over death. Even as Christ arose from the grave, so shall we rise to meet Him in the air on the last day.

Chaplain: Therefore, we are confident in believing that there is nothing in all of creation which will be able to separate us from the love of God which is in Christ Jesus, our Lord.

Benediction

Chaplain Charles Grooms
Ceremony of Flag Mall Dedication,
Florence, SC
Courtesy of CSM Carlton Pridgen

✝

Chapter Sixteen:

ABOUT THE AUTHOR

Charles Grooms was born the son of a young 21-year-old father and a 16-year-old mother. His father was born and raised in a small, poor Southern textile town in the lower part of South Carolina, and his mother was raised, since age three, along with four other sisters, in an orphanage home in a poverty-stricken section of northwest Georgia. At fifteen years old she was able to leave the orphanage home and go live with her older sister in Bamberg, South Carolina. She met a young man, and married him. And, as fast as nature would take her course, three boys were birthed into the world, Charles being the oldest. At 27 years old, his father died suddenly of complicated kidney problems and left his mother to raise three children, aged three, four and five. Placement of her children in an orphanage was definitely out of the question for her. She made a pledge to her children to spare them of that misery, and she did. She immediately went to work in the local textile mill and, with the help of her father-in-law and mother-in-law, she joined the "textile mill-hill culture." Working to have a better lifestyle is not what drives "mill-hill" folks into the factories; survival is what drives them. Being poor was not a disease, it was a way of life!

This is the author's record of survival and what it takes to be an overcomer. Thanks goes out to his mom for showing her family the true meaning of surviving a hard life. She drilled in each of her children that we should have faith in God, obey our parents, show respect to our elders, give a day's work for a day's pay, strive to obtain a better way of life, and be honest in all things. Also, I owe a lot to my mom's sister and her husband, Bill and Maggie Bunch; they allowed me to live with them for three to four years. In addition, I wish to thank another aunt, my dad's sister, for allowing me to live with she and Grandmother for two to three years. Her name was Mary Pearl. During these years of moving from one home to another, I avoided living all of my youth in an alcoholic environment. In 1944 my mother married a man that was an alcoholic WWII veteran . . . very abusive to my brothers and me.

Thanks, Mom! I have tried to follow your example. I worked hard just like you.

Vocational Experience:

Retired May 12, 1995: 30 years law enforcement career under the S.C. Police Officer's Retirement System. Served as a S.C. Highway Patrolman (four years), Chief of Police (two years), S.C. Dept. of Corrections' Warden (sixteen years), Deputy Director of County Detention Center (six years), and Project Director of County Juvenile Services (two years).

Retired June 24, 1996: Ordained Minister 34 years (evangelist and pastor).

International Pentecostal Holiness Church (website: *www.iphc.org*). Continues to serve as Interim Pastor—June 1996 until the present time.

Teaching Experience: (Criminal Justice Subjects)

S.C. Criminal Justice Academy (1977-80)

Florence-Darlington Technical College, Florence, S.C. (1976-1988)

Chesterfield-Marlboro Technical College, Cheraw, S.C. (1976-1988)

Education

I dropped out of high school at the age fifteen to work in a local textile mill to assist my mother in supporting our family. The reason for this was that my dad died twelve years earlier and left my mother with three small children to support; I was the oldest at age five. Also, my stepfather was an alcoholic . . . didn't work much and she needed some help.

Upon reaching the age of 17, I enlisted for three years in the U.S. Marine Corps. Combat training was completed and orders were issued to go to Korea. The Korean Conflict ceasefire order was given, necessitating a change of orders. I was reassigned to Military Police duty at Cinclant Fleet Headquarters, NATO Command, Norfolk, Virginia. I served in this command until enlistment was completed in May 1956. After serving three years on active duty, I served another six years in the U.S.M.C. Reserve. My reserve duty was completed in 1962.

Upon returning home from the military service, jobs were hard to find so I reentered high school under the G.I. Bill, not for the education, but to get financial help. At 21 years old, I returned to high school to seek my high school diploma. I picked up where I left off six years earlier by entering the ninth grade. I started dating a high school senior, not for love or sex—but for English and math help. However, we fell in love and a year later we were married.

She graduated and I again dropped out of high school to support my family. However, my wife encouraged me to take the South Carolina high school GED test. I did. I passed the test and received my high school diploma.

One of the greatest decisions I made was to become a Christian. I stopped my wild lifestyle in April 1962 and was converted, "born again." I joined the church, and later studied to become a Sunday school teacher. A year later I was elected a deacon of my church, the Bamberg Pentecostal Holiness Church. In 1964 I organized a Boys Club (see photo, page 205) and on May 13, 1964 I received my minister's license to preach. God has been good to me.

After having served three years in the US Marine Corps, I found out that discipline was one of the ingredients in my life that I really did not get, as I grew up without a father. I needed discipline, plus, I needed someone who cared for me, and would show me the right way to go. Shortly after I was converted and joined the church, I organized a Boy's Club. I tried to show love, compassion and provide things for each of them to participate in (camping, baseball/softball, trips, et cetera), especially reach out to those boys who had no father in the home. I knew how that was; I had experienced that growing up. Plus, I set it up similar to a military command with a taste of discipline to make it interesting and enjoyable to be a member. It worked out very good. My pastor, Rev. Sam Pressley, assisted me in every way to make it work . . . to him I give a lot of the credit for its success.

At the age of 34, after serving four years as a S.C. Highway Patrolman, I received the spiritual calling to become a minister. To prepare myself for the ministry, I made a decision to continue to improve my education by

My First Command
Boy's Club—Bamberg, SC—1963
Photo courtesy of Joel Hand

To the right is my pastor, Rev. Sam Pressly (deceased). To the left side from the top down are young men that assisted me with the boys. They are: Bobby Blume; H. M. Grooms, my younger brother (deceased); Raymond Mitchum (deceased); Rev. H. Larry Jones, a cousin; Pee Wee "Cooper" Gunnells (retired). Cooper was one of my 14-year-old 9th grade classmates; I was 21; and myself at the bottom.

The Boy's Club members, beginning at the top left to right, are: Dennis Bell, Dennis Black, Tony Still, Sammie Bunch, Steve Jones, Terry Still, Sonny Bowen, Randall Jones, Steve Haddock, Jimmy Jones, Randy Bowen, Frank Smith, Terry Bowen, Robert Bunch, Steve Bowen, Herbert Rudd, Daniel Rudd, Dean Haddock, Greg Bowen, Eric Brabham, Eric Pressley and Pee Wee Smith. Members not shown in the picture are Odell Bunch (deceased), John O'Neal, Robert Sweatman, Todd Bridges, Glenn Ward, Mark Ward and Tim Still. We had over 45 members; I have forgotten their names. A reunion is being planned.

entering college. In 1969, at the age of 34, I became a fresh-man in college with the assistance of my veteran's benefits under the G.I. Bill. I attended college year-round until I completed the requirements to graduate and earn my accredited degrees:

AA degree in Police Administration, Midland Technical College (1973)

AA degree in Correctional Administration, Midland Technical College (1973)

BA degree in Biblical Studies, Southwestern College (1975)

MA degree in Biblical Studies, Baptist Christian University (1978)

Doctor of Ministry degree, Corel Ridge Baptist University (2000)

Other colleges/universities attended: Emanuel College, University of Georgia and University of Colorado (1969-1980).

Veteran and Military Career

U.S.M.C. Veteran (PFC): Reduced in rank two times, plus served two 20-day sentences in a military brig for being AWOL (drinking/partying—lost track of time). However, during the same period, I earned Marine of the Quarter honors. I was good, then not-so-good. Thank the Lord He rescued me before I got strung out! I served three years active duty (1953-56) and six years as a U.S.M.C. Reserve (1956-62).

South Carolina Military Department
    Office of the S.C. Adjutant General
    South Carolina State Guard
    Chaplain: 15 years (1983-98)

Commissioned as Captain and promoted up to Colonel.

Positions served were: Battalion Chaplain, Brigade Chaplain, Deputy Staff Chaplain for Administration, Deputy Staff Chaplain for Operation, Plans and Training, Deputy Staff Chaplain for Pastoral Care, Deputy Chief of Chaplains, and Chief of Chaplains.

Joint Services Detachment

Chaplain Advisor for Religious Affairs: 12/98-4/2001

Promoted to Brigadier General: 12/21/98

Transferred to the Joint Services Detachment, office of the adjutant general, as Chaplain Advisor for Religious Affairs (served as JSD Staff Chaplain and performed chaplain-related duties as directed).

Assigned tasks:

1. Plan and organize a chaplain program at the South Carolina National Guard-sponsored Youth Challenge Academy (YCA), and provide a weekly scheduled chapel service, counseling and mentoring assistance to staff and cadets. (The program was established, and is continuing as an important and viable part of the YCA program.) A staff of chaplains were recruited, trained and assigned to continue the chaplain program. The YCA program began its third year of existence in January 2001. It has become one of the top priorities for the adjutant general (TAG).

2. Serve on the S.C. Military Museum Committee.

3. Assist in establishing a statewide YCA Mentor Program.

4. Serve as TAG's Official Program Evaluator of the YCA Mentor Program. The objectives are to:

   • establish Regional Mentor Coordinators,
   • assist with recruitment of community mentors, and
   • coordinate mentor training.

*Military Schools/Management/Leadership
Schools/Training*

> *U.S.A.F. Air University:*
> U.S.A.F. Chaplain Counselor Course
> Chaplain Staff College, Regional CAP (1983-1997)
> Ft Belvoir, VA
> Ft Mead, MD
> Dover AFB, DE
>
> *S.C. State Guard and U.S.A. Officer Training School*:
> Command and Staff Procedures
> Federal Emergency Management
> Unified Direction of Armed Forces
> Gas Mask Containment
> Reserve Components
> Med-Center Air Team Program
> Assertive Management
>
> *S.C. Criminal Justice Academy*:
> S.C. Highway Patrol School
> Correctional Officer Certification
> Correctional Officer Supervisor Certification
> Weapon Qualification (pistol and shotgun)
> Other administrative training
>
> *University of Georgia*:
> School of Drug Abuse and Alcohol Studies
> Role of Corrections in Communities
>
> *University of Colorado Academy of Corrections*:
> Correctional Upper-Level Management
> Correctional Management
>
> *Management Consultants/S.C. Criminal Justice Acad.:*
> Assertive Management II
> Budget Grievances
> Motivation
> Personnel Management

Problem Solving
Prison Accreditation Honor: First S.C. warden to have a
    nationally accredited prison under the standards of
    the American Correctional Association

State Guard Association of the United States (SGAUS)
National Chaplain Staff College—Griggs University
National Chaplain Staff College Graduate (1995-2000)
Military Funeral
Critical Incident Stress Management

Awards and Decorations
National Defense Ribbon
Cold War Meritorious Medal
U.S.M.C. Commemorative Medal
Exceptional Service Medal
Distinguished Service Medal
Medal of Merit with two OLC
Federal Service School Ribbon
Longevity Service Medal with one OLC
Service Ribbon with two Silver and three Bronze Stars
Achievement Ribbon
Volunteer Service Training Ribbon
Military Readiness Ribbon
Recruiting Achievement Ribbon
Military Proficiency Ribbon
Governor's Unit Citation
Commendation Medal
Meritorious Service Medal
SGAUS Recruiting Ribbon
National Service Award
National Chaplain Executive Committee Citation
National Staff College Graduate Ribbon with four
    Bronze Stars
SGAUS Life Member Ribbon with one Silver and one
    Bronze Star
National Chaplain Unit Citation

Individual Achievement Ribbon
Distinguished Service Medal
National President Texas Meritorious Service Medal
The Jewish War Veterans' National Americanism and
    Patriotism Medal (Received in 1997; one of a few
    Christian chaplains to receive this award.)

Note: Upon retiring from the chaplaincy on April 13, 2001 (27 years of military service), the S.C. adjutant general awarded TAG's highest medal, the Exceptional Service Medal. Also, the SGAUS awarded their Distinguished Service Medal and a Certificate of Commendation.

The Exceptional Service Medal reads as follows:

> The Exceptional Service Medal is presented to Chaplain (Brig. Gen.) Charles E. Grooms, Joint Services Detachment for exceptional meritorious service while serving as chaplain of the Joint Services Detachment and Coordinator of the Mentor Program of the Youth Challenge Academy. Chaplain Grooms' efforts in getting the Youth Challenge program on track and his tireless work in getting services and benefits to veterans have been exemplary. Chaplain Grooms' patriotism and dedication to the moral principles, which made this country great, reflect his character of service to his state and nation. He is highly commended, and his service has set the example for all that may follow.

From 1998 to 2001—6 April 2001

Signed by Major General Stanhope S. Spears, The S.C. Adjutant General

State Guard Association of the United States
National Chaplain (Served four consecutive years, 1995-1999)
National Executive Committee
National Chaplain Emeritus for Life (10/2000)
During 1995-1999, as National Chaplain, the following were planned, studied and established. They were:

- The office of the National Chaplain.
- National Chaplain Executive Committee was established and initiated, consisting of twelve different denominations being represented to break down the barriers of noncommunication between chaplains of different religious faiths.
- Staff study for establishing a Chaplain Staff College under the office of the National Chaplain (the Chaplain Staff College was implemented in 1996).The first graduation occurred in 1996, and has continued to be conducted in subsequent years.
- Election criteria for electing the National Chaplain and officers of established committees.
- Established a National Chaplain Council consisting of past National Chaplains (they serve as advisers to the office of the National Chaplain).
- National Association of Veterans Outreach Ministries (NAVOM): Chaplain (Brig. Gen.) Charles Grooms— Founder and Chief Executive Officer.

Visit our website at:
www.veteransoutreachministry.com (official ministry site)
Email: *cgrooms1@sc.rr.com*

The NAVOM was officially founded on November 11, 2000, and was established as an outreach ministry to veterans and their families. The association was placed on the World Wide Web on December 1, 2000 (*www.veteransoutreachministry.com*) as a "church without walls" primarily to reach out to "unchurched and unsaved" veterans, their families and others. An invitation is extended to *all* religious faiths, churches, veteran organizations, independent ministries and businesses to become associate members and help establish a united effort to help our veterans and their families.

All churches and civic organizations that do not have an outreach ministry in place to reach out to veterans are encouraged to *start* one. Also, we recommend that each church and/or civic organization plan and conduct an annual event to recognize veterans in their church/organization and within their communities.

The ministry has been: (a) approved by the South Carolina Secretary of State as a nonprofit, tax-exempt religious organization; (b) issued a Federal ID number; and (c) the process is underway to apply for and receive approval under federal guidelines for 501c3. The long-range plans are to build a veterans' chapel (Chapel of Refuge), an administrative/training complex, homeless shelters, a cafeteria (to serve one hot meal daily), a gift shop, and an overnight motor home parking site to accommodate association partners and visitors. Tentative plans are underway to begin a fundraiser to build the complex on a plot of land on I-95 in Florence County, S.C. Please consider partnering with the NAVOM to reach our homeless and needy veterans. Please visit our website for more information.

Florence National Cemetery
Mrs. Susie Powers, widow of MSGT John Powers, USAF Retired.

Sgt. D.W. Garner, 78 years old and a personal friend
World War II 101st Airborne Veteran

Annual Training—AT96
(L-R) WO3 Jack Williams and Chaplain Grooms

✟

WORKS CITED

1. Heichelheim, Fritz. *A History of the Roman People.* Englewood Cliffs, N.J.: Prentice-Hall, Inc., 1962. pp.420-435.

2. Fanning, William H. "Chaplain." *New Advent: Catholic Encyclopedia.* Vol. III. New York, 1908 *http://newadvent.org/Cathen/03579b.html*

3. Matz, Terry. "Saint Martin of Tours: Patron of Soldiers." *Catholic Online Saints*: 1966 *http://saints.catholic.org/saints/martintours.html*

4. Ramsey, David. "Life of George Washington." *http://Early Americans.com*

5. Ibid.,4.

6. Nettles, Curtis. "George Washington." *Encyclopedia Americana. http://gi.grolier.com/presidents/ea/bios/01pwash.html*

7. Ibid., 4.

8. Ibid., 5.

9. Ibid., 6-8.

10. Ibid., 10-11.

11. Ibid., 12.

12. Ibid., 13.

13. Ibid., 14-16.

14. Ibid., 17.

15. U.S. Constitution

16. U.S. Code, Title 10.

17. Army Regulations 165-1. *Chaplain Activities in the United States Army*. Washington, D.C.: Government Printing Office, 1998.

18. *http://www.germantown.K12.il.us/html/deaths/html*

19. U.S., Department of the Army. "Chaplain Activities in the United States Army" Army Regulations 165-1. Washington, D.C.: Government Printing Office, 1998.

20. Army Regulations 165-20. *Duties of Chaplains and Responsibilities of Commanders*. Washington, D.C.: Government Printing Office, 1983.

21. S.C. State Guard. "Office of the Chief of Chaplains." *Standard Operating Procedures: Chaplains*. Columbia, S.C.: Government Printing Office, 1983.

22. S.C. State Guard Regulations. "Military Funerals." *Standard Operating Procedures: Chaplains*. Columbia, S.C.: Government Printing Office, 1983.